ROUTLEDGE LIBRARY EDITIONS: SCOTLAND

Volume 21

IS SCOTLAND EDUCATED?

IS SCOTLAND EDUCATED?

A. S. NEILL

LONDON AND NEW YORK

First published in 1936 by George Routledge & Sons Ltd.

This edition first published in 2022
by Routledge
2 Park Square, Milton Park, Abingdon, Oxon OX14 4RN

and by Routledge
605 Third Avenue, New York, NY 10158

Routledge is an imprint of the Taylor & Francis Group, an informa business

© Original 1936 Edition 1936 & 2021 The Estate of A. S. Neill
This new facsimile and e-book editions © 2021 The Estate of A. S. Neill

All rights reserved. No part of this book may be reprinted or reproduced or utilised in any form or by any electronic, mechanical, or other means, now known or hereafter invented, including photocopying and recording, or in any information storage or retrieval system, without permission in writing from the publishers.

Trademark notice: Product or corporate names may be trademarks or registered trademarks, and are used only for identification and explanation without intent to infringe.

British Library Cataloguing in Publication Data
A catalogue record for this book is available from the British Library

ISBN: 978-1-03-206184-9 (Set)
ISBN: 978-1-00-321338-3 (Set) (ebk)
ISBN: 978-1-03-207589-1 (Volume 21) (hbk)
ISBN: 978-1-03-207626-3 (Volume 21) (pbk)
ISBN: 978-1-00-320796-2 (Volume 21) (ebk)

DOI: 10.4324/9781003207962

Publisher's Note
The publisher has gone to great lengths to ensure the quality of this reprint but points out that some imperfections in the original copies may be apparent.

Disclaimer
The publisher has made every effort to trace copyright holders and would welcome correspondence from those they have been unable to trace.

IS SCOTLAND EDUCATED?

by

A. S. NEILL

GEORGE ROUTLEDGE
AND SONS, LTD. Broadway
House, Carter Lane, London, E.C.
1936

First published 1936

PRINTED IN GREAT BRITAIN BY THE EDINBURGH PRESS, EDINBURGH AND LONDON

CONTENTS

	PAGE
I. INTRODUCTION	1
II. THE SUBJECT	11
III. SCOTS LEARNING	18
IV. CREATION AND POSSESSION	36
V. THE KIRK AND EDUCATION	48
VI. EDUCATION AND SEX	64
VII. SCOTS HUMOUR AND EDUCATION	86
VIII. EDINBURGH AND ST ANDREWS	93
IX. THE RURAL SCHOOL	109
X. THE SCOTS WHO FLED	127
XI. PSYCHOLOGY IN SCOTLAND	138
XII. SCOTLAND AND THE ENGLISH LANGUAGE	160
XIII. HEALTH, MANNERS, AND DISCIPLINE	173
XIV. THE FUTURE	182
XV. BOOK REVIEW	189

I
INTRODUCTION

To write a book on Scotland and Education is for me a difficult work. My qualifications for this work are few, and my disqualifications are many. Chief among these is a lack of interest in the historical: I am only interested in today and tomorrow, but chiefly today. In my time I have read historians like Hume Brown and Andrew Lang, finding them, of course, prejudiced in their outlook as all historians must be. Just the other day a book was published with the title *Scotland's Suppressed History*, by M. E. M. Donaldson. Its historical objective appears to be to show that Scottish history has favoured the Presbyterians at the expense of the Episcopalians. I began to read it with interest, and when in the middle of the book the authoress told of a Scottish lady, who in 1644 was suspected of witchcraft and " forced to stand dressed in sackcloth, in one place, and for twenty-six days not allowed to sit down, and being

INTRODUCTION

kept awake all the time," I accepted this as good history: but when the authoress added in parenthesis: "Here we have a far from isolated example of the Covenanters forestalling the Bolshevik methods of the Metropolitan-Vickers' trial in Moscow," I knew that her "history" was just as biased as any history of mine would be, and, no doubt childishly, I did not read the rest of the book. I say childishly because the lady has as much right to have a prejudice against Moscow as I have to have one in favour of Moscow. But we are in the same boat in this way, that our "histories" are coloured by our personal complexes.

Hence all I can write about Scotland will be rather gaudily coloured by my prejudices against Scotland . . . and to some degree by my prejudices in favour of the Scots. Also naturally coloured by my own sense of insufficiency and failure. That is no fault: no man can ever be objective, and the man who says he can see both sides of a question is a dull dog and a danger to society. The only possible method of finding out the truth is to hear the biased opinions of both sides, that is, if the truth concerns people and nations: the method does not apply to the truth that water is composed of oxygen and hydrogen, although it is possible that one day some scientist

INTRODUCTION

will find that water has a radium or a vitamin Z component. We cannot get the truth about people because we are people. All we can know of the emotions comes from our supposition that other people have exactly the same emotions as we have, and, to some degree, this might be called a safe rule-of-thumb method, for if I sit down on a pin my reaction will be similar in appearance, if not in verbal expression, to that of the Archbishop of Canterbury if he sits down on a pin. The illustration shows life at its simplest. If, however, we make the illustration a little more complex we are in difficulties. Taking the Moscow trial just mentioned, why should my attitude to it be different from that of—say—Winston Churchill? The answer is that whereas sitting on a pin appeals (or rather does not appeal) to one's primitive sense of comfort, the Moscow Trial stirs up a million complexes that environment has formed. Winston Churchill believes honestly that Capitalism is good: I believe honestly that it is a curse. Nor is it a case of wisdom and ignorance. I am just as wise as he is. Our knowledge differs, of course: in a debate on economics he would possibly tie me into knots, but in a debate on psychology I should possibly leave him at the post. It is not knowledge that

INTRODUCTION

counts: it is prejudice, that is, something emotional and, be it confessed, frail. If I were to meet Winston Churchill I feel sure I should like him, and that he would like me. In fact I nearly wrote him recently asking for an interview . . . but my motive was utilitarian, for as an amateur bricklayer I wanted to compare mistakes with another amateur bricklayer.

It seems impossible then that anyone can write a good history. We grow daily, hourly, and, if a historian's opinions are the same at the end of his book as they were at the beginning, he is a dead man. This accounts for the frequent charge of inconsistency that is so often levelled against writers and politicians. Growth implies inconsistency. That is why I always consider a boy an inferior when he says that he knows what he wants to be in life: there is the extreme danger that he has crystallized out at too early an age. No man of whatever age should know what he is going to be in life. I have a poor opinion of Robert Louis Stevenson, but I like his truth that it is better to travel than to arrive. The goal is always a disillusionment. Success is a childish longing realized and found to be an empty bauble. Like many another man, I set out to get fame and wealth. I got neither, but I realized in the effort to attain them that

INTRODUCTION

they were valueless. Sour grapes? I do not think so. Everything in life comes too late, said Jerome K. Jerome. It is partly true. If at the age of twenty-five I could have seen my name in *Who's Who*, I should have been very proud indeed. I do not say that today I am entirely indifferent to the fact that my name is in *Who's Who*, but it gives me no special thrill, nor did its first appearance inspire me to go out and celebrate it with a binge. It is the same with titles. In our younger days we value them, overvalue them, but as we grow older we do not find peace in the phantasy that we appear in the King's Birthday List. Twenty years ago I should have rejoiced if my name had suddenly become Sir Alexander Neill, Bart., yet today if the State decided to reward me for my work in education by offering to make me Lord Summerhill, I should refuse the honour. Honours in Britain have something sinister and ugly about them. I always think they lower a man's status, and that is because the Honours racket is a dirty one, tainted by gold and political intrigue. I have often wondered why brilliant surgeons and artists accept knighthoods in a system that makes profiteers barons. Still more do I wonder why Labour officials take titles from a capitalist civilization.

INTRODUCTION

But we are all snobs, and in our hearts we climb to upper circles. The only difference between a Labour Lord and me is that our interpretations of snobbery are different, and our respective ideals about upper circles are far apart from each other.

If a man wants wealth he will get it. It is true for most men who are not born in a Glasgow slum. Most of us, thank God, do not in our hearts value wealth, and this is especially true of Scotsmen. Scots meanness covers a contempt for wealth. It is not so true that the Scot despises fame, yet the fact that few Scots acquire a world fame is significant. The Scot seeks fame among his own folks. He wants to impress the people of his own wee village or sma toon. He may take a broad view of history, but he takes a narrow view of geography.

I fear I am a Scot with a narrow view of history and a broad view of geography. I know that the publishers might have got any one of a score of Scottish educationalists to write a good book on Scottish education, yet there is a slight advantage in my writing the book, the advantage of seeing Scotland from afar. True, much of the detail is lost in a far blink: one cannot see the trees for wood. On the other hand the trees do not darken one's writing-

INTRODUCTION

room window. In either case, whether Scotland is seen by a resident or an emigrant, it is seen with a squint. And by each Scottish education is seen with one eye. How can I judge Scottish education when that education helped me to judgment? No slum-born man can look at the slums with an aristocratic eye: to the shoemaker there is nothing like leather, because he lives with and smells leather all day long, but his bairns are the worst shod, because, deep down in his soul, he hates leather. So to some degree every man hates his education, for he attaches his sense of frustration to it. . . . " If I had been educated elsewhere! Then I might have succeeded where I have failed." Possibly all of us look back to cross-roads and wonder what would have happened if we had taken the other road. I was once offered two jobs by the same post. I chose one. Had I chosen the other my career would have been entirely different in environment, friendship, love, hate. Yet in my heart I know that I would have been the same person in all essentials. Like the people in Barrie's *Dear Brutus*, our second chances would prove that our faults, and our fates, are in ourselves.

There is one thing that puzzles me in writing. In life I am an easy-going person with a temper that is

INTRODUCTION

difficult to lose: I have no enemies among people I have met (although strangers who have heard of my work call me terrible names): I can suffer fools gladly . . . yet I find that in thinking about Scottish education I have angry emotions, and I feel sure that in these pages I shall say a few bitter things. I have puzzled a lot over this apparent Jekyll and Hydeish business of living and writing. I have much enjoyment in Ethel Mannin's sense of humour when I converse with her, but I cannot find her humour appearing in her books. The explanation is that writing betrays the other part of our egos. No satirist is so full of spite as his books are; no sermon writer so good (or so bad) as his sermons. I am told that the most bloodthirsty thrillers are written by timid, small, thin men who live in fear of their wives. Our books are our over-compensations in life, and it may be that our books on good and moral behaviour are written by villains of the deepest dye. Yes, they must be.

Hence every book is a lie. It betrays the worst side of the author. A man cannot psycho-analyse himself because he over-emphasizes his bad points, and a book is an attempt at self-analysis . . . and always an unsuccessful attempt at that. George Douglas Brown did not solve his Œdipus Complex

INTRODUCTION

when he made himself, in the form of young Gourlay, bash his father's head in with a poker: he could not possibly solve it because old John Gourlay was also a symbol of himself. All characters in a novel or a play represent various parts of the author's personality. Shakespeare was Hamlet, but he was also Hamlet's uncle and Hamlet's mother, yes, and Poor Yorick too.

So that in this book I shall be Burns and Knox and the Kirk and scores of other factors. When I praise Burns, as I hope I shall, I shall be rejoicing in what joy of life I possess: when I anathematize Knox, as I fear I shall, I shall be disapproving of the remnants of Calvinism that lie buried in my unconscious memory. And, alas, my readers will be just as subjective. They will agree with me when their complexes favour my complexes, and they will disagree violently when my complexes tread on the corns of their complexes. To some I shall be a good fellow who knows what he is writing about, to others I shall be a blatant egocentric fool . . . but there is a slight satisfaction in knowing that my worst critics will be those who have the same faults as I have. We hate in others what we are trying to repress in ourselves.

Every man has a King Charles's head, but the head keeps changing from day to day. My King Charles's

INTRODUCTION

head at present is possession, and that possession is represented by the possessive system we call Capitalism. My preoccupation with Capitalism is not a political one; rather is it a psychological one. I am convinced that there is no hope for humanity so long as possession defeats creation, so long as things are valued more than human souls. Scotland is a Capitalist country, and its educational system must be one that favours the continuance of the present economic system. My views on Scottish education, therefore, will be coloured by my views on the system of which it is a part. Another writer might have Latin or Physics as a King Charles's head: another Mr Dick might see Scottish education as a background to Sir Walter Scott or James Maxton or to the bagpipes. That does not matter if the reader is prepared for what he is about to receive, whether he is truly thankful or not. The reader ought never to be deceived. The author should lay all his cards on the table, yes, even the cards he has up his sleeve. The opening words of every book should be: This book is going to be a narrow-minded treatise by a prejudiced author. . . .

So now I can go on with a clear conscience to a subjective and biased dissertation on Scotland and its Education.

II
THE SUBJECT

WHAT has education meant for Scotland? How can we answer when we have not defined our terms? What is Scotland? Today Scotland is a suburb of London. Today education is . . . but that I cannot define. If education is learning then Scotland is educated, but if education is creation then Scotland is uneducated. And if education means culture Scotland is barbaric.

The most obvious line to take is to interpret the word education as the average teacher or doctor or lawyer in Edinburgh would interpret it: that is, to use it as a definition for schooling and university training. And from this angle let us shout aloud that Scotland is a well-educated land with more than its share of M.A.'s and W.S.'s. Scottish schools are good and Scottish universities are good. If the Leaving Certificate is something of value; if an M.A. Degree is worth more than the parchment that lends it a dignified value, then there is nothing to be said but: Heil, Scotia!

This book will attempt to give my reasons for

refraining from saluting my native land with a Heil! The land I would salute at any time. It is a fine country. Its folk have guts and manners and much friendliness. Compared with England it is a sincere country; it has little use for servility and the bastard manners we call etiquette. The character of the Scot is something to be proud of . . . but then any Swede or German would say the same about his own countrymen. Patriotism is a thing of reality when it is real love of country, but when patriotism is the tawdry thing that waves flags and seeks militarism, it is only an exploitation by the ruling class of something that is originally good and worthy.

Love of country is a widened love of the family home. Our deepest loves belong to childhood, and modern psychology shows that most of our later loves and hates are repetitions of the early love and hate of childhood. In other words our intellects grow, but our emotions remain childish or rather childlike. It is the child in a man that is the patriot. A true patriot lives for his country, whereas the patriot who dies for his country is the victim of a trick. A man dies for the enemies of his country—the financiers, the imperialists, the armament makers, the profiteers, the exploiters, *i.e.* his rulers.

THE SUBJECT

I am no true patriot. Instead of living for my country I live in England, not for England but for my work. My work is in education (whatever that may be), and I cannot work in Scotland because Scotland has little interest in education. In fifteen years I have had only four Scots pupils. Every year my school has scores of visitors, teachers from the Colonies, Germany, Norway, Sweden, America, but seldom does a Scots teacher come to see what is going on. (As I write I think of the visitors I have had this week . . . nine Swedes, four Norwegians, two Germans, a Dutchman, and at least ten Colonials. . . . I do not regret that Scots have not increased the number.) Scots aren't as a rule so easily taken in as more simple nationals are. It is indeed difficult to teach a Scot anything. I recall a meeting I had with rather a prominent Scot a few years ago. He had expressed a desire to meet me, and a meeting was duly arranged. He clasped my hand fervently.

"Man, Maister Neill," he said, "you're the wan man I have wanted to meet. You are an expert in education, and I just want to hear you enlarge on the subject."

He paused while he paid for the drinks.

"As I see the matter," he went on, "the main thing in education is so . . ." and for an hour he

THE SUBJECT

talked education. I had nothing to say. My contribution to the talk was an occasional: "I see" or "Yes." When he left he shook my hand warmly.

"Man," he said, "I haven't enjoyed a conversation so much for a long time."

Now this man was no dunce nor was he a fool. He knew many things that I was ignorant of; he was a clever botanist for one thing; he was a good historian for another. But he knew nothing about education, while I knew quite a lot. Why then did he tell me his views instead of asking me for mine? Possibly the most reasonable explanation is that the Scot suffers from an inferiority complex that originates in the smallness of the land. The Scot does not like the fellow-Scot who emigrates, and when he meets him he attempts to show the emigrant that the man who stayed at home is just as good or perhaps a little better. The most depressed Scot in the world is he who, returning to the North after some success in the South, expects recognition of his worth. The wise Scot creeps back to his native town in old clothes and a cloak of modesty. Long ago I entered a small shop in Kirriemuir. The name over the door was Barrie. To the goodwife I said: "Are you any relation to J. M. Barrie?"

THE SUBJECT

"I am," she said shortly, "but I'm no' proud of it." But of course she was proud of it. We are indeed a queer lot o' fowk.

My own native town tries hard to show that it does not know who I am. A year or two ago I entered a shop in my native town. The shopkeeper kept eyeing me as he tied up my parcel.

"Ye'll be ane o' the Neills?" he said agreeably.

"Ay," I nodded.

"Oh, ay," he went on pleasantly, "ye'll be the minister?"

"No," I replied, "I'm not the minister."

He studied me a little more intently.

"Then ye'll be the doacter?"

I shook my head.

He smacked his lips, gave me a pitying look, and said: "Oh, I see, then you'll be the lad that writes books?"

He knew from my entrance that I was the lad that writes books. Like the man who wanted to hear my views on education, he knew how to keep me in my place. George Douglas Brown would have classed him as a nasty Scot, but that would be an unjust description. He was a good fellow behaving in the normal Scottish way.

THE SUBJECT

I have few illusions about myself. I have done some hard work in child psychology and have written a few books that are not high-class literature. I can get a packed hall when I lecture in London, Oslo or Stockholm, but the local papers in my own county seldom mention my name. Recently when I was lecturing in Oslo a questioner asked me: "Why is a prophet never acknowledged in his own country?"

I answered: "Because it knows him too well."

The burst of laughter was so tremendous that I thought I had struck some great truth . . . then my chairman told me that the laughter had nothing to do with me; my questioner was a devout follower of a minor prophet in Norway. Apparently Norway also knows how to treat its minor prophets in the right way.

The aggressive egoism (and egotism) so often found in Scotland comes no doubt from the geographical situation of Scotland. I called it a London suburb. I might have called it a province or a nationality tinged with the B.B.C. accent. If a country has no Home Rule you may be sure it does not want Home Rule. Not that Home Rule would make a scrap of difference to Scotland; the rulers (finance, monopoly capital, vested interests, etc.) would simply make Edinburgh their headquarters instead of Westminster. In political matters Scotland is nowhere. It accepts the English rule with due servility, and, when London pulls the imperial strings, the docile Scot forms fours and marches to fight for the all-powerful master—imperial capitalism. Scotland is loyal, but not to Scotland.

Of course I agree that the English or the French or the Germans obey the call of monopoly capitalism in the same way as the Scots do, only they are benighted folks who have not had the advantage of the much praised educational system of Scotland. Why have a land where M.A.'s are common as dogs going barefoot if it is no more advanced politically than less lucky lands? The sad truth is that Scots education is of no value whatever so far as anything that matters in life is concerned. An M.A. is no more educated than a bricklayer. (I am at the moment spending my afternoons bricklaying, and feel strongly that I'd sell my M.A. parchment willingly for the ability to keep a wall straight and perpendicular.) Scots education is mere learning, book learning at that, and learning is one of the things humanity could well do without.

As I seem to be touching on many things without solving anything, I shall proceed to take the several items separately. To begin with this business of learning.

III
SCOTS LEARNING

SCOTLAND has hitched her wagon to two minor stars—the M.A. degree and the Leaving Certificate. When a headmaster in the North showed me over his rebuilt school some time ago, I said: " All very nice. Now show me the workshop."

" The what? " he asked in surprise.

" The workshop," I said.

" We haven't got a workshop," he said with some impatience, and added: " What has a workshop got to do with education? "

Scotland is filled with fine elementary and secondary schools which turn out many more or less learned youths, but these schools do not give education: they give book learning. I say more or less learned youths, for although they may know Trigonometry up to the solution of triangles, and the history of Britain and the rainfall of Timbuctoo, they are hopelessly ignorant of all that is embraced in the word Kultur. They know nothing of music, painting, sculpture, sex, politics, economics, civics, literature.

I am not over-emphasizing the importance of what is called Kultur. A Parisian sculptor may be as uneducated as a St Andrews M.A., B.D. Well, perhaps I should say as unlearned, for if true education is mainly associated with creation, the sculptor is the better educated of the two. And true education is creation, doing not absorbing. Knowing is of comparatively little importance. In the important things of life we do not act by knowing or thinking; no man can fall in love by taking thought. Emotion is beyond thought and learning, and emotion rules our lives. I once knew a Scots girl who had taken the Higher Leavings with honours in analytical geometry, but she had the vaguest of notions about how babies were made.

It is an interesting speculation why school subjects came to be considered as educative. Practical utility they have not. Ancient languages have no utility, and to most people no interest. Modern languages have utility only if one travels or reads foreign books, but the modern languages we learn at school sink into the forgotten and usually remain there. Most students after years of French can ask haltingly the way to the

SCOTS LEARNING

Arc de Triomphe, and most of them cannot understand the answer that the gendarme gives. Mathematics have (or has . . . have sounds better) about the same value as a crossword puzzle, and much less interest. From the practical point of view they help but little. Since leaving school I have never had occasion to do a long division sum in money, or a cube root, or any sum dealing with acres, roods, poles, gills, pecks; I have never had to rack my brains over A, B, and C who are alleged to do a piece of work in so many days; I have never had to ask myself how long a train takes to pass a signal box, nor how long a man will take to row upstream. The only fractions I use are to be found on a foot-rule, and decimals never seem to appear on my horizon. And if these so-called practical things are useless to me, how much more useless are x's and y's and equations!

History . . . ah, this is a controversial matter. How can man live and progress if he does not know what other men have done before his time? I suppose that is the chief reason why we teach children the causes of the Hundred Years War, or what Charles II said on his deathbed. The history taught in schools is the history of all that does not matter in the past.

There might be some value in teaching children the history of labour from early serfdom to the dole, but teachers dare not teach such dangerous history: history must be safe. Our schools are conditioned and regulated by the State. The State is a capitalist, imperialist State, apparently ruled by a sham democracy, but in reality ruled by the minority who hold the power and wealth. The schools must not therefore teach anything that might be subversive of this State. Like the daily press, the school history book must not say a single thing that matters, and, like the press, the history book seeks always to further the propaganda that the ruling class wants to disseminate. Hence to call the Boer War an outrageous piece of aggressive imperialism would be intolerable; hence to describe the Great Civil War of 1914–18 as a battle between two rival groups of imperialists would be very bad taste.

In any case I challenge the view that to know of the past is necessarily of any help in planning the future. If it were true then we should elect our history professors to be our rulers. If I found myself studying Rousseau and Pestalozzi and Montessori I should give up my job as a failure. To be a good mason one does not require to learn the history of masonry. If a man wants to study history let him read the thousands of books on the subject, but to force children to study history is simply stupid.

So far as book learning is concerned the only things necessary are reading, writing, and counting numbers. The rest is ballyhoo (I don't know what the English translation of ballyhoo is: it might be bunk).

Scotland, by making its education book learning, has damned itself effectively. It has become smug about its education. Here's to oor eddication: wha has an eddication like it? The answer is, unfortunately, that the whole world has eddication like it, only other countries are not all content to rest on their educational oars as Scotland does. Other nations have their pioneer schools. Scotland, provincial Scotland, is outwith the current of modern experiment.

True, I speak as an outsider who has little opportunity of seeing what is really going on in Scotland, but today my copy of *The New Era* dealing with education in Scotland has just arrived, and I note that such an authority as Dr William Boyd writes as follows: " The outstanding impression is of vitality rather than of progress, of steady strenuous work going on everywhere *rather than of educational adventure* (mine the italics). . . . There is rather more experi-

SCOTS LEARNING

ment in the south and more readiness to try new ventures on the part of a small but increasing body of teachers, but on the whole the Scottish teacher is very slow to move where innovations are concerned. . . . Not many small schools and still fewer big schools have got the length of abolishing either home lessons or corporal punishment."

Boyd goes on to say : " The absence of experiment, however, is obviously not due to any lack of keenness about education. There Scotland stands where she stood. Rather it is the outcome of the temperament of the Scot who wants to move forward but takes no risks."

Boyd is so good in this article that I must quote him further. After stating the sad fact that nothing seems to be doing in the Infant School, he goes on to quote a critic of the Secondary School, who says : " Nothing new is happening or can happen in the secondary schools in spite of the fact that they are staffed by honours graduates. Initiative is almost completely strangled by the Leaving Certificate."

Now, what William Boyd says is worth paying attention to. In the same number of *The New Era* he tells of how he came to modify and change his attitude to education in general. He is a man who has stayed

SCOTS LEARNING

at home, and it would appear that his studied observation of Scots education agrees in large part with my unstudied feelings about that education. From this writing of his I gather that there are a few explorers in Scotland, but that the great majority are (to quote him) "a fine group, but canny, very canny." Canny, yes; I prefer the word provincial. And, to be just, there are thousands of teachers in other parts of the world who are but canny, very canny. No doubt I expect too much from Scotland and the Scots, the Scots who of old held up their heads in independence, whose sons went out and succeeded among less energetic and progressive peoples.

This copy of *The New Era* that I have with me now is a Scottish number. Several teachers write articles about how they are conducting new experiments in education. Good articles in the main; good teachers with some vision. But the main body of teachers is unprogressive and unimaginative. They accept the education system of the Scottish Education Office as easily as they accept the rotten system of living that we call civilization. Even the Scots pioneers have to trouble about teaching the children things, of course, for within a system one cannot be too pioneerish. My contention is that Scots teachers believe in the bunkum they have to teach; they believe in school subjects and textbooks. They " want to go forward but take no risks " (Boyd). Oh, no, if a man won't take risks about what he believes in, be sure that he doesn't believe in it. Scottish teachers accept the system not because they are compelled to, but because they want to retain it. It is not easy for a specialist with an Honours Degree to face the truth that his subject may not matter a damn in the scheme of life. Pioneering is too difficult if its result is to be a job lost. To the shoemaker there is nothing like leather . . . and apparently to the Scottish schoolmaster also.

I am an impatient sort of a fellow, and one of my complexes is an anti-marking-time one. Another is a hate of compromise. I want to have a new world by magic, so to say, and it makes me sad to find people struggling with compromise things like Dalton Plans and pseudo-self-government schemes. Hence it is but fair to say again that I look at Scotland with prejudiced eyes. I want it to get a move on because I love it. I want it to lead instead of following. And it does follow. The articles in *The New Era* I have just mentioned are over twenty years late in appearing. They should belong to the time when Edmond Holmes and Caldwell Cook and Norman MacMunn were writing of their new experiments. None of them is as arresting and as original as the new educational methods of E. F. O'Neill nearly twenty years ago. It isn't modesty that keeps me from including myself in the list. As a Scot, of course, I am a better man than any of them, but I claim no original experimentation in education, because education is a thing that doesn't interest me . . . school education, I mean. All I have done has been to prove that a school doesn't need to be a school. And my objection to Scots schools is that they are schools.

I hasten to add that if Scotland has avoided new ideas in education, she has at the same time avoided going crazy over bleak systems like the Montessorian system with its pre-Freudian psychology. It is indeed strange that Scotland did not take Montessorianism to its bosom. The land of Knox and the Sabbath might well have adopted the psychological Puritanism and "rationalism" of Madam Montessori, with its emphasis on duty and order and intellect and reason. The Montessorian dread of emotion should have appealed to the repressions of the Scottish middle class; the delights of the pedagogical apparatus should have delighted the dominies who love Long Division; the catholicism of the system's creator should have fitted in with the puritanical catholicism of the Scot. But the sad truth is that Scotland did not refuse to take up Montessori because it hated her system, but because it never heard of her system. This comes from the fact that Scotland is a suburb of London. The fashions come late to the more remote suburbs.

It is true that Scotland is suburbia. The Edinburgh flapper who talks of " taking the ' care ' from Murrayfield to the Meound " is doing the correct thing; she is modelling her language on what she supposes to be good English. And a good suburbanite will always seek the standards of the West End. To be Englified is the ambition of all Scottish West Ends, and our speech bewrayeth us. I speak not as one superior to linguistic weakness. I speak " English " with a Scots accent. I have often rationalized the motive, saying to myself that if I talked about a girrrrrrl or a birrrrd the poor southerners would not understand me. A pure rationalization, of course, for Harry Lauder's broadest Scots is easily understood in the south. The real reason why I speak in a compromise manner . . . that is one that is between " Oaverrr therrre " and " Ovah thah " . . . is that I was nurtured in a Scotland where, even in the last years of last century, the standard of speech and fashion was England. In school every Scots child speaks English, but in the playground he or she speaks dialect. As the son of a dominie I had to speak English in the house, but I spoke broad Forfarshire with my mates, and, to this day, I marvel how slickly I changed over from one to the other when I entered my home. Yet we must remember that there is more in the question of dialect than the aping of the superior English; there is the equally important social question. To speak dialect is to betray your belonging to the lower orders, that is the orders who do most of the work in life.

Outwardly, Scottish education may appear to be a relatively classless one. In a town of the size of Forfar the lawyer's son will sit in class beside the son of the sweep, and, be it said, feels no snobbery about it either. The best families, of course, send their sons to English Prep and Public Schools either in England or in Scotland, for our Scottish Public Schools are essentially English in character and tradition. Having seen neither of them, I conjecture that Eton and Glenalmond do not differ in any way in essentials; their products are the same products . . . they both turn out Public School Men . . . and that's that. So far as I can gather, our Scottish Public Schools have much less bearing on Scottish life than the English

Public Schools have on English life. There are groups of folk in the south who like to ask you what school you were at, and if you weren't educated at one of the " Big Four " you feel a little embarrassed in answering, but I never heard anyone in Scotland ask a man what school he came from. In the north we have not the damnable division between the gentleman and the mere man that the south has. We are a much better folk with much more self-respect. Why, it always comes as a delightful surprise to me, when I cross the border into Scotland, that the people aren't gaping for tips. If a ploughman in Fifeshire offered me a lift in his cart I should never dream of tipping him, but if I get a lift down south I fidget about the size of the tip the man will expect.

Men are nearer equality one with another up north . . . yet when I think of my residence in Newport, Fife, many years ago I almost doubt my own verdict. Newport in those days was Scotland in miniature. Sons and daughters of rich houses sat in school beside sons and daughters of the milkman and the lamplighter. But the parents of the rich children did not invite the children of the poor to their Christmas parties. Newport had its grades of society, and the highest grade was difficult of entry. Once in the grade you were safe . . . until you lost your money and had to earn a living. I remember one young lady whose father went bankrupt, and she had to go out and earn her money as a typist. She was automatically cut out of the invitation list of the topnotchers.

The Newport men were not snobs. In the daily train journey to Dundee they hobnobbed irrespective of social standing. As in all other places, it was the women who made the social standards, and, although I thought one of them beautiful and charming, I must confess that the women of Newport were as bleak a lot intellectually and culturally as one can find in any outlying province. Most of them toiled not, neither did they spin . . . because many of their men were jute spinners in Dundee. Money was the chief standard in Newport thirty years ago. Culture was almost non-existent and, what there was, was the kind of culture that rhapsodizes about the inferior qualities of a Gilbert and Sullivan operetta. After all, it is unwise to expect more from wholesale and retail trade.

My chief recollection of " society " in Newport and other Scots towns is one of long, boring conversations about ailments and trips. Scots folk are tremendous egotists. They will tell you tiresome details about how they missed the boat at Gourock, and what

Aunt Mary said, and how Uncle Angus lost the tickets. Usually they preface the description with the words: " Oh, it was awfully funny." It never was and never is. Scots have a fine sense of humour, but it seldom becomes apparent in " society " circles.

In its favour I must say that the " society " of a Scots suburb has no illusions about a university education. An M.A. is of no value in Newport if he hasn't got a bank balance. A sound principle indeed. A bank balance means some constructive work generally, but an M.A. is only a man who has learned a few things that are fundamentally of little or no value. It is the lower and lower middle classes up north that put an exaggerated value on university training. What has happened in Scotland has been that the really efficient men made money, and in their hearts despised the miserable devils who wanted an academic career. Money-making in Scotland was one of the few vices that were tolerated. Spending money meant wine and women and all the other vices, so that the only vice left was to make more and more money.

When I was fourteen I became ambitious. I wanted to be an M.A. I had only the learning that a village school affords, and I resolved to attend classes in the

SCOTS LEARNING

Heriot-Watt Institute in Edinburgh, an institute in which aspiring youth could learn the road to success. I recall standing at the door one night and watching the tutors enter the building, and the thought struck me: "These men are to help me to succeed, but look at them! Most of them look miserable, badly dressed, in short the opposite of success." I was right. There is no success in an academic career. It is a second best, a sop to the lower middle classes who can never reach the real success of wealth. And I almost ask myself the question: "Did old Andra Carnegie realize this when he offered Scotland free university fees? Did he try to sidetrack youth into worthless academic degrees so as to keep the rewards of capitalism for the few who were above such a conception of success?" No, I do not think he did. Carnegie sprang from the lower class, and in all likelihood he retained to the end the lower class illusion that a university man is somebody of importance.

Very few people realize that our university men and women are in reality underlings. In a capitalistic society they are nobodies. Whether they enter law or medicine or the kirk or teaching they are servants who have to carry out the plans of their masters . . . the men who make money. And they have the servant mentality : thus they pride themselves on their convervatism, not realizing that a conservative must be a dead person. To put it in modern psychological terms, in terms of the Œdipus Complex, a conservative is a man who accepts the father as a god who is always right, while the left-winger is a man who challenges the rightness of the father. And since the law of growth says that the father is never in the right, the young conservative is living in a dead age . . . the age of his father's youth.

Our Scots universities are conservative of the right (Tory) or of the left (Liberal). Psychologically there is no difference between a Tory and a Liberal : both support capitalism and the Old Men of life. Our professional classes, university trained, show much less originality and intelligence in political matters than our Clydeside workers show. That is mainly because a university training does not deal with fundamentals. It is a surface thing dealing with the intellect and neglecting the emotions almost entirely. It is almost wholly uncreative. I find professors and university lecturers in the aggregate the dullest of company, pedantic, timid, conservative, consciously inferior. Dimly they must realize the inferiority of their job, for it is an inferior job to serve a master like monopoly capital. Capitalism very cleverly selects the brighter children of the proletariat, sends them to secondary schools and then to the university, thus taking them away from the class to which they belong and for which they might conceivably fight, and turning them into castrated black-coated servants of capitalism.

I admit the excellence of our Scots universities in teaching students to be specialists. A university training in Edinburgh or Glasgow is in no way inferior to a training in Oxford or Cambridge. My contention, however, is that a specialist is not necessarily an educated man. Harley Street specialists sometimes advise parents to treat their children in a way that is barbaric. You can teach a subject but you cannot teach life in a university. Any university tends to be behind the times. A professor of psychology recently admitted to me that " perhaps there was something in Freud." When I took my English course in Edinburgh, Professor Saintsbury always stopped short at Walter Pater. The reason he gave was that any writer more modern came within the province of controversy. I am told of a Midland university where the staff simply dare not express left-wing views, because the university receives grants from the industrialists. Only in Cambridge apparently dare a professor or don go out and wave a red flag in a labour demonstration.

Why is not a university like that of Glasgow leading the workers to a better civilization? Why do students as a class become blacklegs in a strike? The answer is that our university system is tolerated and supported by the powers that be only when it is an obedient servant to those powers.

Scottish education is a bulwark of entrenched capitalism, and instead of being proud of it we should raise our voices against its subservience and reaction.

IV
CREATION AND POSSESSION

CREATION and possession are innate in everyone. Possession which commences in mother's womb seeks ever to be safe and static: its ultimate goal is the security of death. Creation is life itself, movement, love, joy, happiness. When a man achieves creation he is fully alive, but when he anchors himself to possession he is spiritually dead.

And now I ask the question: Is Scotland creative or possessive? Have we a great Scots literature or art. If we have, I haven't seen it. What we do have is an engineering greatness, but whether that greatness is one of creation or only construction I do not know. There are conclusions we arrive at by intuition yet cannot explain by reason. Just as I feel that Communism is the economic form of the Mother Complex while Fascism is attached to the Father Complex, so I feel that Scottish engineering is a form of Calvinism. Similarly I feel that the Oxford Group movement is the religious side of Fascism, but I cannot give an intellectual proof of this feeling.

CREATION AND POSSESSION

Generalizations are hopeless things. Scotland, like every other land, has creative individuals and possessive individuals. And there are few occasions on which we can definitely say that such and such a crowd is creative. We can say it today of Russia where the masses are building a new civilization, but can we say it of the masses of the old civilization? Capitalism is possession at its zenith, and we may safely believe that under capitalism creation will be held to be subordinate to profit-making. To return to my illustration of Newport, Fife, possession governed most things. The making of money and its concomitant, the keeping up of appearances, ruled out Kultur. A better example might be Edinburgh, beautiful Edinburgh, with its tradition of East Windie and West Endie. Just as Newport or Broughty Ferry contrast with the slums of Dundee, so does Murrayfield contrast with the wretched Cowgate. English towns have their slums, to be sure, but I have never seen slums so miserable as in Dundee and Glasgow. Possibly slums strike one forcibly in Scotland because of the innate feeling of equality among men that the Scots have. Industrialism and slums have not killed that inner something in the Scot that is a man, that national independence and pride of race.

CREATION AND POSSESSION

I have just returned from a motor tour of the Highlands, and again I have been delighted with the people I met. I have no illusions about the exploited Highlands with their tartan racket and their gentleman servants' attitude to their lords and masters the English capitalists. I was addressed as "Sir" in Inverness, but not in Melrose. When a girl in a tobacco shop in Glasgow said to me: "Ye'll be on holiday?" I realized that I was being treated as an equal by an equal. And I was being treated as one human being should treat another, in a classless way. I know of no other part of these isles where servility is less than in lowland Scotland. In the north of Scotland one feels that the people have been made unreal, that there is too much of the gamekeeper flunkey in the folk psychology. This was bound to follow the robbery of the peasant and the turning of his land into deer forests. Thus in writing about education in Scotland I must think of the Lowlands, for northern Scotland should form a sub-chapter in a book about the English Public Schools.

Scotland is not a creative country. Obviously no creative country would value the Higher Leaving Certificate or an M.A. degree. No creative country would have so obscene an attitude to creative sex as

CREATION AND POSSESSION

Scotland has. The uncreative Scots Sabbath is enough to damn any nation for ever, and Calvinism, which still lives, is the negation of creation; it is possession de luxe . . . save your own miserable soul and get your reward hereafter. Just as the multitude chose Barabbas, so the Scots chose John Knox.

But I do not contend that the Scot is not creative. He is . . . in his unconscious. Consider the Robbie Burns cult. Burns was a creator. He sang of the joy of life; he lived in a way that was the antithesis of Calvinism. To this day Burns means much to the Scot; there are Burns suppers, but I never heard of a Knox supper. Burns lived in a way that every Scot lives in his phantasy, that is, Burns represents the repressed unconscious of Scotland. Now the unconscious is creative and instinctive and joyful. Calvinism attempts to kill the instinctive strivings of the folk, but Calvinism cannot kill those strivings, it can only suppress them. The Scots do not admire Burns because he wrote lovely lyrics: few of them are able to distinguish between a Burns song and a song by Harry Lauder. They admire Burns because he said and did all the things that they have wanted to do themselves. Robert Burns is the national unconscious, the creation that Calvinism dammed up at birth. At a Burns supper, therefore, the whisky must flow, because it is only through the releasing of repressions by drink that the Scot can get into touch with his unconscious longings. The more advanced Scot, like the Forfarshire ploughman, does not need the help of whisky to enhance the charm of that creative ballad *The Ball of Kirriemuir*, but then the true proletariat is always less repressed than the bourgeoisie. In Scotland, as in all other lands, the middle class is dead . . . paradoxically enough, for it is a parasitic class and parasites are usually over lively.

It must be accepted as a psychological fact that the unconscious life of a people is much more important than the conscious life. The jokes about Scots meanness have their source in the repressed life of the Scot rather than in the circumstance that Scotland is a poor land whose inhabitants must of necessity be canny with their siller. Other poor lands have no reputation for meanness, nor am I convinced that Scotland is so poor a land as folks say. From the Borders to Nairn is a triangle of fine farming land with occasional wastes that should be forest land. When we have a Socialist civilization Scotland should become a Norway for trees; under a system which depends on profit-making planting trees is too slow a method of making money.

CREATION AND POSSESSION

The meanness of the Scot lies in the meanness of his soul. When I stayed a night in Nairn last week and watched the sombre-clad folks creeping to kirk, summoned by a woeful bell, it struck me that the soul of Scotland was mean and narrow and wretched. But this impression has only the value that attaches itself to a complex, for a kirk bell takes me back to the miseries of youth, with its long sermons and dull hymns and psalms.

In Nairn the thought came to me: Suppose the Jacobites had won! The Stewarts were corrupt and valueless, but Jacobitism had a creative joy about it. Bonny Prince Charlie represented to the Jacobite what Rabbie Burns represents to the modern Scot; he was the symbol of repressed life lived out. My historical knowledge is very weak, but I have a vague idea that, like Rabbie, Charlie died a drunkard. This is no place to enter into the difficult task of explaining the psychology of drunkenness, but it is interesting to note that a drunkard is a man whose infantile repressions have overcome him: like every babe, he is fond of his bottle. He seeks in drink the fulfilment of his phantasies. George Douglas Brown, who lived before much was known of psychology, gave a brilliant picture of the drunkard in young John Gourlay, the weakling whose phantasy life overwhelmed his conscious life. Burns was conquered by puritanism in the end: he disapproved so much of his joy of life that he fled to whisky and death. Life is creation: death is possession.

Scotland is a death country. The most vivid memories of my boyhood are unhealthy memories of death—of burials and black clothes, of hearses with plumes, of lightnings that were to strike young sinners down, of cuts that were to make one die writhingly of lockjaw. Scotland revels in death. I have not seen another country with so great a pleasant interest in funerals. Not long ago, when a Scots merchant was showing me his new car, he pointed out its chief merit straightaway. "Man," he said, "it'll do a funeral in top gear." In Scotland a man's social value is not made manifest until his funeral day; the length of the procession is his obituary notice; the size of his tombstone determines his importance. In Scotland you retain your social position after death, and in the cemeteries the rich refuse to lie beside the poor. It may be so in other lands, but I never noticed class distinctions in a German or Swedish cemetery.

I recognize that Scotland's interest in death is in part due to its scant population. In a village a death

CREATION AND POSSESSION

is an event, while in a city a death is a localized affair. There is more in it than that, however. Scotland hugs death to its heart because Scottish life seeks death. Calvinism was death, for it was the negation of joy. Calvinism was accepted by Scotland because it fitted into the psychology of the Scot, the death-seeking psychology. But to answer the question: Why did Scotland acquire a death-seeking psychology? is a complicated business. Climatic reasons must have played a part. When recently, in giving a lecture in Oslo, I remarked that it was dangerous to teach a child religion, half a dozen headmistresses got up and walked out of the hall. And in Norway I found black clothes and the equivalent of the Scots Sabbath. Lack of sun and warmth produces what I call death psychology. In symbolism the airts have a definite meaning: going West, as popular language knows, signifies death: going East is rebirth—going to the rising sun: going South means life and joy: going North always denotes a desire for the coldness of death. There is nothing strange about this. Life is hard in the North; vegetation grows with difficulty: life is a struggle, and the facilities for joy are few. Since the sun is the source of life and joy, it cannot be expected that a comparatively sunless land like Scotland will be a joyous land. The night in dream symbolism often represents death, and in Scotland the nights are long. Still the nights in Greenland are longer, and I have never heard the Eskimos described as a death-seeking people, so that the climatic explanation is not enough.

We must consider, then, the political and economic factors also. Generally speaking, the history of Scotland is one of internal strife followed by poverty. According to my old friend J. B. Salmond, Editor of *The Scots Magazine*, the Highland Chiefs were the forerunners of the Chicago gangsters. Rob Roy appears to have out-Caponed Al centuries before Al was born, and the woes of Scotland right down to Culloden appear to have been due to the fact that gangsters are very bad collaborators. I see Scotland of the Middle Ages as a kind of early Abyssinia, but I cannot decide which of the then gangsters was a Mussolini . . . possibly Robert Bruce filled the bill most fittingly. Right through the ages Scotland was full of war and death, and when Calvinism came along, a tired and weary people, acquainted with physical death, gladly accepted the spiritual death that Calvinism offered them.

The economic factor possibly played the chief role in predetermining Calvinism. The history of Scotland is one of poverty and exploitation. Long before the

CREATION AND POSSESSION

exploitation of the Industrial Revolution the poverty of the masses was appalling. My grandfather, who must have died before the middle of the nineteeth century, kept a family on fourteen shillings a week, and that would almost appear to be affluence when we read old records of miserable payments made to labourers and schoolmasters. Calvinism came with its promise of a new life in death, and as the folk were without the means to enjoy life they very easily accepted the pessimism of predestination and hell. Hell has always been popular in Scotland because it was no strange place: Scots life was hell.

Again, Scotland was off the map. That was a salient factor. It had (and has) the narrowness of vision that accompanies being off the map. As Calvinism came as a relief from internecine strife and insecurity to Scotland, so to England came Puritanism as an antidote to the license of Tudor England. But today Puritanism in England is much weaker than Puritanism in Wales and Scotland. An outlying part is bound to be parochial. Talk to a man who has lived in India or British Guiana for years and you will almost surely find him dully parochial and narrow. I am fairly alert at this moment, yet I know that if I were to become headmaster of a village school I should, in six months, be running to pull back the kitchen blind to see where Mrs Broon was going.

It is little wonder that with such a history and environment the Scot has become immortalized as a canny fellow. Canny means thinking many times before you act, and the Scot certainly thinks. Thought, however, is a late-comer in human life, and it is consequently an unimportant acquisition. It is a dangerous acquisition, for thought, if it cannot add one cubit to a man's stature, can stunt his growth in spiritual things, and by spiritual things I mean creative, instinctive things. The thoughts of Burns and Shakespeare were trite things. Turn into prose any one of Shakespeare's great soliloquies and you find them commonplace. "To be or not to be", "All the world's a stage". Shakespeare's philosophy is of no real value: it was his glorious poetry and character drawing that made him immortal. So it was Burns's poetry and love of life that gave him immortality. And no one can love life or write great poetry by taking thought. Creation comes first and it uses thought as it uses ink or paint . . . as a servant.

The canny Scot deified thought, introducing it even into his long dull sermons. Roman Catholicism, which fears thought, has not lost much of its hold, whereas

CREATION AND POSSESSION

the "rational" Protestantism has been dying for two generations. Personally I abominate Catholicism more than I abominate Calvinism, for it prostitutes the emotions and changes creative joy into hate and fear. (I have just got a new pupil from a Convent School, and she tells me she had to bath herself in a chemise in case she saw her own naked body. She is ten.) No, Calvinism may prostitute thought, but the crime is venial: to prostitute God's emotion is one of the vilest of crimes.

We see clearly the Scottish devotion to and belief in thought when we return to consider the popularity of education. The schools teach children to think, not to do. I have more than once written that the chief function of any school should be to prevent children from thinking ... and got labelled as a paradoxist for saying so. It is no paradox. Thought is necessary: thought is even of value: but if the emotions are starved and stunted, thought is only a dangerous curse. The man who called James the First the wisest fool in Christendom was a wise man. Our schools and universities are filled with James the Firsts. The curse of Scotland is thought. To be fair, however, I must add that the Germans beat the Scots in their insane worship of thought. Hitler must be the Nemesis.

V
THE KIRK AND EDUCATION

SCOTTISH education began in the kirk. The first schools were kirk schools, and the first teachers were monks and priests. Grant's *History of the Burgh Schools* and Jessop's *Education in Angus* tell the wretched story of the influence of the kirk on education in Scotland. The teacher was a servant of the kirk, and no ungodly man was allowed to deal with the young. It is probable that many teachers were stickit ministers, and there is evidence that the school was used as a jumping off platform for the pulpit. For generations the ambition of every Scots mother was to see her son wag his pow in the pulpit. My own mother had this ambition, and my eldest brother became a minister. I also set out to enter the kirk, and only the fortunate realization that I was too religious prevented my entering the ministry also.

It is many years since I sat in a Scots kirk, and in recent years religion in the north may have progressed. Yet when I read in my paper that Provost Murray of

THE KIRK AND EDUCATION

Dornoch has been practically excommunicated because he allowed dancing in his house until two a.m. I hae my doots. This regression to the infantilism of the Reformation sounds Gilbertian: like the rustic who saw a giraffe I feel inclined to cry: Hell, I don't believe it! For it is almost incredible that Scots religion can be so insane as Dornoch appears to make it. If the Scots kirk were alive its ministers would rise in a body and declare that the Dornoch decision was the negation of all religion, but I question if the Scots kirk ever was alive. It certainly has kept a heavy dead hand on poor Scotland. Allied in its temporal power with the robber barons and exploiters, it still retains the baronial attitude, now that it has lost much of its temporal power. The familiar saying that the *Church Year Book* was the young minister's Bible was no joke: the most interesting part of a parish to the minister is the stipend. There are, of course, individual ministers who are beyond the primary interest in a stipend: I speak of the kirk as a whole, the repressive, possessive Scots kirk.

The history of the Scots kirk has been one of the ugliest stories in history. Its cruelty in the past was simply devilish. It had neither love nor charity: it was a hate institution. Just as Provost Murray of

Dornoch has been chastized by the local haters, so was Scotland of the seventeenth and eighteenth centuries turned into a hate country by the hatred of the kirk. Christ was a lover, but Paul was a hater. The Scots kirk followed Paul, who certainly would have supported the punishing of a lad for whistling on the Sabbath Day. Paul, who said the most beautiful things about charity, had no charity in himself; he hated the flesh and he hated women; he turned the loving message of Jesus into the hateful gospel of Christianity, a gospel that was to produce the Inquisition and the boot and the thumbscrew and the Scots Sabbath. The Sermon on the Mount was set aside for the Apostle's Creed, and the lovable, loving Jesus became the foundation of a Christianity that was disciplinarian, militaristic, hateful, dead. It is the grimmest joke in history this perversion and exploitation of Jesus. That so beautiful a character should be the foundation of a Scots kirk with its prosy sermons and ugly dark architecture and Sunday fashions and emptiness of spirit is a tragicomedy. The tragedy of any hero's life is this, that you can make your hero what you will. In the New Testament Jesus is an impossible contradictory character. He is full of love and charity, and he preaches hell fire and damnation on the next page. The men who wrote the Gospels obviously coloured him with their own psychology. Thus the kirk had the choice of two characters. It chose the Barabbas version of Jesus, just as it chose Knox instead of Burns.

It is significant that the Scots kirk values words more than it values deeds. When a living is vacant, applications for the post are sent in, as in all other businesses and professions. A leet is drawn up, and this is then narrowed down to a short leet . . . often determined by wangling. The individuals on the short leet are then invited to preach on consecutive Sundays, and the congregation then decides by vote. The candidate is judged by his sermon. I have known a parish in which a brilliant sermon saddled a congregation for twenty years with a minister it disliked intensely. Words are words and nothing more in the realm of religion. Religion is a matter of feeling, not of intellect or dialectics. Really there is nothing to be said about religion, but there is much to do about it. But the Scots kirk, being far away from true religion, accepted the Word as a standard, and, having control of lay education, made talking and thinking the important things in the schools. So long as the pastors of any kirk are members of one class—

the middle-class—there can be no religion of any value in the State. Jesus was poor, with no sense of possession and without ambition, and no follower of Christ can live in a manse with comparative luxury. You can't love your neighbour as yourself when he touches his cap to you and respects you. I do not pretend to be above luxury for one moment. Ministers as a class are not too well paid, and, as individuals, no one will grudge them their comfort. My only objection to them is that they are serving two masters— Jesus and their middle-class status. But then I hold the view that Jesus does not need ministers, that the kirk is superfluous and long out of date. The life of Jesus cannot be interpreted by anyone: his love and inspiration appeal to the heart and not the head that Scots sermons talk to.

Modern psychology with its discovery of the unconscious has knocked the bottom out of Christianity as we know it. Just as little Willie can give his conscious attention to mathematics while his unconscious interest is in killing Red Indians, so can his father stand up in the kirk and sing *Abide with me* while his unconscious is God knows where. Hymns, like sermons, are words, and like some sermons some hymns are made up of platitudinous nothings. There is very

THE KIRK AND EDUCATION

little poetry in the Scottish Hymnal: it is sad to think that the religion that inspired the building of Milan Cathedral also inspired the words and music of the average hymn or anthem, or for that matter the architecture of a Scots kirk. I suppose that when Milan Cathedral was built religion was in its right place . . . it was unconscious, whereas the dull Scots kirk came at a time when religion had become a matter of reason and thought and argument.

What is wrong with the Scots kirk is its inability to recognize that Burns was much nearer to Jesus than Knox was. If there is such a place as Heaven you may be sure that Rabbie is joyfully strumming his harp, while John Knox is grousing about Mary Queen of Scots' sex appeal in her rather modern angelic gowns. And I think that Paul is supporting him.

Jesus was what we make him. My own impression of him is a simple one. I discount as unessential all stories of his miraculous birth and his equally miraculous resurrection. Such stories belong to the wish fulfilment of the race. The hero must not be as other men: he must be the son of a god, and he must never die. The resurrection myth attaches itself to heroes in general. Hector Macdonald was seen in Scotland after his death: Gordon of Khartoum, Kitchener, and in recent weeks Lawrence of Arabia have lived after death. In the case of Jesus it is of no importance to humanity whether he was miraculously born or not. His resurrection is of no value to religion. It was what happened between his birth and his death that matters. The important thing is that Jesus lived for sinners, not that he died for sinners.

I see him as a simple man who loved life. That he left his carpentry was perhaps a pity, for it is better to do than to teach. And if he had stuck to his bench we might have been saved the iniquity of the kirk. A disciple is always wrong, and it should be the desire of every man to have no disciples. Discipleship seems to involve hate, and the bitterest quarrels are those between fellow-disciples. A hint of this is seen in the antagonism among the disciples of D. H. Lawrence: each one seems to be convinced that he or she alone knows the truth about the Master. We see similar antagonisms among the followers of Freud. However, the fact that the disciples of Jesus perverted his message does not affect the original message. His message was that the chief aim of life should be to love, that is to give creative love rather than to receive possessive love. In his simplicity of soul he, of course, did not realize that disciples, in the garb of churchmen, would in the twentieth century interpret their Master's conception of love in a manner that allowed them to bless battleships, or that his love of life and humanity would ultimately lead to the insane chant of the churches that we are all miserable sinners. Jesus did not believe in sin . . . Oh, yes, I know that he said: "go and sin no more," but I am writing about the character of Jesus, not about what he is reported as having said. Only narrow little miserable wretches can believe in sin. There is no sin. Jesus knew it because his intuition was great: we know it through the more elaborate process of psychology. A boy often steals because he is unloved: he steals symbolically the love that his parents never gave him. He has no control over his actions because the unconscious desire to be loved is infinitely stronger than the wish to be social. The one way to cure such a boy is to give him love. Thus modern psychology has only discovered a profound truth that Jesus knew two thousand years ago. But his kirk has never known it. It has judged and condemned. Dornoch's condemnation is merely comic, but the kirk as a whole has never stepped in to rescue the young thief from the " Christian " justice of our out-of-date and barbaric law courts.

THE KIRK AND EDUCATION

Jesus judged not, but his kirk has judged much. Think of its obscene attitude to the human body. Think of its depressing attitude to pleasure. A kirk that believes that it is more holy to sit and listen to prayers which direct the Almighty, than to kick a tennis ball along a country road on the Sabbath, is a kirk that has neither religion nor any sense of human psychology. In fact such a kirk does not know what religion is. Religion is loving, and in what way kicking a ball or dancing a foxtrot on a Sunday lessens lovingness I cannot see. Ministers do not smoke in public . . . curiously enough they smoke in railway carriages and on railway platforms: they do not enter public houses and drink with their parishioners: they never swear—in public: they only go to music halls in Assembly Week. Their lives are intended to be an example to their flocks. Poor wretches, it isn't their fault; they are the victims of a scheme that accepted the gospel of love only to exploit it in the interests of the powers that be in the State. For it is in the interest of the ruling classes that the humble classes should be kept subservient and sinful and moral.

This is the kirk that has had so potent an influence on Scottish education. I have not painted it nearly

THE KIRK AND EDUCATION

so black as I could because my intention is not to throw mud; my intention is rather to scrape off some of the mud that has got attached to Scots religion. It is impossible to have a free healthy education in a land that is kirk-ridden. Calvinism and Roman Catholicism have this in common, that they insist on interfering in education, and in both cases the interference is soul-destroying. It was the kirk that demanded of the underpaid, hard-worked dominie that he should teach religion in the school, and in many cases the school was in a parish where the minister had little to do all the week. I have seldom met a Scots teacher who did not resent having to do the minister's work in this way. In my schooldays I recall my father's having to cram us in Scripture because a local minister was commissioned by the School Board to inspect us, and this was at a time when my father's salary depended on his grant, and his grant depended on the number of duffers he could persuade to pass Standard V. But the Scripture Lesson had to be given before ten o'clock, that is before the register was marked. H.M. Inspectors were apparently of the opinion that religion wasn't a part of education. That is the only compliment I have ever paid the H.M.I.

THE KIRK AND EDUCATION

It was not only in the schools that the kirk influenced education. It encouraged children to learn during the week and then, on Sunday, it discouraged them from being alive. It interfered in behaviour, and preached hell and damnation for the erring. I admit that in recent years it has dropped its hell component, quite illogically, for if one drops hell one has some difficulty in defending one's retention of heaven. The kirk attempted to keep its flock on the narrow road, and it therefore had to act as a censor of morals. Dornoch forward!

I recall a Scots story.

Macgregor had been to kirk and on his way back Tamson was standing at his yaird gate.

"Aye, man, Geordie," said Tamson, "ye'll hae been to the kirk? What was the munister on the day?"

"Man," said Macgregor, "he was on fornication."

"Imphm," said Tamson, "and what sort o' a line did he tak?"

"Man," said Mac with the air of giving surprising news, "man," he said, "he was against it."

I have never understood why Mac was surprised. Personally I never had the luck to hear a minister on fornication: the kirks I attended were much more vague, thundering against possible sins of commission and omission. It is an alarming fact that fornication only becomes a sin when you have a kirk or an equivalent suppressive moral body. As the law makes the crime, the kirk makes the sin. The kirk must make the body sinful, because it believes that the spirit is of greater value than the body. Fornication is condemned not because it is sinful but because it is pleasant.

It is a strange factor in Scots religious life that one goes to kirk all dressed up (often because one has nowhere else to go). If the body is vile why dress it so carefully before you enter the house of God? The conscious motive probably is that you have to look your best when you seek the Lord, that thus you show your respect for the Almighty. But I am glad to say that the unconscious human motive adapted Sunday clothes to its own purpose, and made the kirk the fashion parade of the week. When I was a child I could never see the pulpit for fashionable enormous hats . . . but I cannot recollect being bothered at not seeing the pulpit. What did bother me as a child was the sartorial Sunday morning preparation for church, when I had to have my hair oiled and my cuffs fixed on, and when I had to wear boots that gave me corns for life. Indeed I wonder

THE KIRK AND EDUCATION

how much of my anti-kirk complex springs from those boots. Much more likely the roots of my complex come from the wretched Sundays of my childhood, when going to the kirk was tolerable, mainly because staying at home meant prohibition of walks or games or fun of any kind. Later on, when I reached the fashion plate interest, I went to church to show off my clothes, and incidentally to give glad eyes to the alluring damsels in the choir. In some obscure way religion and sex are closely allied, and, after all, it is pleasant to know that many love affairs begin in the kirk, for it proves that human nature will bring love into the most loveless places.

It is a debatable point whether Scots who leave Scotland are actuated by ambition or by the desire to fly from the dullness of the Scots kirks and schools and the narrowness that is associated with them. I have never met an Anglicized Scot who expressed a wish to return to his native land to live there. We love to visit our country: we never doubt the fact that a Scot is better than ten Englishmen: we never lose our accents and we retain our sense of humour. We have no illusions about England, but on the other hand we lose any illusions we had about Scotland. A Sunday in London is almost as dull as a Sunday in

Edinburgh, but not quite so bleak: you can get a drink in any English town without being a *bona fide* traveller for instance: you can dance or play golf without attracting much notice. . . . but I hear you can now play golf in Scotland. The Church of England appears to have much less influence on the life of the people than the kirk up north has. For the past eleven years my pupils have danced every Sunday night to a blaring radiogram, but the local church and the people have made no objection. I tremble to think of what would have happened to us if we had been in Dornoch or Lossiemouth, although it is probable that we could have danced in Glasgow or Edinburgh with impunity. About twenty years ago when I was writing my *Log*, it was reported to me that a local minister was perturbed because he heard my typewriter tapping on a Sunday. A South African Inspector of Schools told me last year that he dare not go for a joy-ride in his car on a Sunday in South Africa. He added: " You see the Scots kirk element has still a strong hold in South Africa."

Dancing and joy-riding belong to the Devil, although if it is true that the Devil has the best tunes, he does not introduce many of them into the dance hall. If he is responsible for the hot rhythm variety his taste is certainly deteriorating badly, but then the poor fellow must be overworked and in consequence careless.

Since the kirk is so interested in the Devil it is fitting to discuss him for a few minutes. There is, of course, no Devil. He is the obverse side of the God coin: he is God made human . . . and lovable. You could classify men according to their respective religious categories. Thus:

GOD (*really the Devil*).	THE DEVIL (*really God*).
Knox.	Burns.
Bishop of London.	George Robey.
Gladstone.	Oscar Wilde.
The Nun.	The Courtesan.
St Paul.	Jesus Christ.

These are what we might term the black and whites: the rest of us are possibly rather dull greys. In terms of psychology God is the conscious and unconscious repressing force (I refer to the God of the kirk), while the Devil is the instinctive happy unconscious of childhood. The glad side of life belongs to the devil . . . the dancing, singing, love side of life. Christianity in its perversion of Christ's message has changed God into the Devil. Ask any child if he would rather go to the cinema or to Sunday School, and the answer will prove the contention that the real God is in the cinema, and the real Devil in the kirk, for the choice of a child is of the greatest value: the child is nearer to God than the adult is, because his instinctive life is less spoiled by hateful moral judgments. That is what Christ meant when he said that we must become as little children if we are to enter the kindom of love. Calvinism worships the Devil, only it calls him God. But no God could have ugly kirks and ugly tunes and ugly doctrines. The Christian God is a devil. God would not have his servants dressed in joyless black—black the symbol of evil and death. A God, who promised life eternal, would not carry his dead in black boxes, and have black-coated ministers intone lugubrious words at gravesides. The attitude of humanity to this perversion of goodness and godness makes one despair of humanity. Goodness does not mean suppression of life's desires: it means approval of life's desires. To approve is to love, and to love is to approve. The Devil loves, and I see no hope for Scotland until she and her kirk go to the Devil.

VI

EDUCATION AND SEX

A BRILLIANT psychologist, Dr Wilhelm Reich, has pointed out that sex repression is unconsciously planned and carried out by the Capitalist class. By suppressing the sex instinct of the workers the ruling class symbolically castrates them, making them docile and unquestioning and unrebellious. This realization of a truth is new, but the evidence for it has long been apparent. The rich have constituted the State, and the franchise of the poor was a mere figment of unreality: the poor had the power to choose between one rich man and another, and when the poor at last set up their own candidates, their Labour bosses were very much of the same mental class as their betters the Tories and Liberals, that is, they were *safe* men, what the Americans would call yes men, men who would not be likely to challenge seriously the State as it existed. And the poor had not the judgment to choose the best men, for the poor were educated in the State schools and given in learning only that which was safe for authority.

Also the rich men made the laws. Law is fundamentally intended to protect property, and the poor have no property. It is not true that in the eyes of the law all men are equal. Lawgivers belong to the possessive class and their judgments cannot avoid being biassed by class consciousness, or it is better to say, class unconsciousness, for a judge is not more dishonest than any other man.

The law aims at keeping the dispossessed in their humble places and here the church proves itself to be a doughty ally. The church has seldom gone against the squire, and it has kept the squire's menials quiet by saying to them in effect: " You do have a rotten life in this world, but do what we say and you will have a pleasant one hereafter."

What happened with property happened also with sex, naturally, because sex involves the sense of property. Morality allied itself to law in order to keep sex down. And morality is the voice of the old men of life who want to keep all the best things for themselves. Such a selfish morality was easy to ally with the selfish religion we call Puritanism. Sex as the greatest of all pleasures had to suffer the greatest of all suppressions in a puritan land like Scotland and the suppression of sex in Scotland must be called obscene, just as all ugly things are obscene. To me *The Ball of Kirriemuir* is not obscene, but when a parish minister solemnly dresses down a couple who have cut their wedding cake before the ceremony (a lovely native idiom) I call that obscenity. I call the Dornoch attitude to dancing obscene. I call the Scots attitude to sex in general obscene. I have seen more so-called obscenities written up on the walls of public lavatories in Scotland than I have seen in half Europe, I say so-called obscenities, for they are the natural re-action to the real obscenity of body—hate and sex suppression, just as *The Ball of Kirriemuir* is the outlet for the healthy sex instinct that the killjoys have warped and stunted.

Consider the matter of swearing. Swearing is of three kinds—religious, sexual, and excremental. The good Scot gets round the religious swearing by euphemism: God becomes " Od, man," or " Michty me ": Christ becomes " Crivvens," and Hell has its own vocabulary of the " Heck " variety. I have seen a stern religious father nonplussed when his daughter of twelve had the inspiration to invent an exclamation: " Cheese's Crust! "

Sexual and excremental words do not lend themselves so readily to euphemism, and their use is usually underground in polite circles, although in rural parts both men and women of the fields show a healthy command of the choicest epithets. That the adjective does not always fit the noun is of no consequence; the main thing is that the rustic betrays his healthy interest in sex in his speech.

Now it is a truth in psychology that we are shocked most by the interests we have most deeply repressed. You must have heard of the maiden lady who complained to the police that a man in the flat opposite did his physical exercises naked each morning. A constable was sent round to investigate. He peered for a long time at the window opposite, and then told the lady that he couldn't see anything.

"But you must put the chair on the table and stand on it," she said helpfully.

I am afraid that the story has some kinship with the Scots subterranean interests in sex and swearing. If we had an open education on sex, half the interest in bad words would disappear; I say half the interest because sex is so important that the most unrepressed person would find its metaphors and phrases springing up in his language. Scotland, which believed so earnestly in the Word, attached an exaggerated importance to the word that was obscene . . . as if what one says matters a damn in life. What does it matter whether Sir Walter Scott swore or not? Only the narrowest of bigots would condemn a man for his language. I remember standing in the square in Cupar, Fife, with my friend and tutor the late Rev. Æneas Gunn Gordon, minister of Kettle. We had waited for the announcement of the parliamentary election result. When it was announced that Asquith had got in by a large majority, a workman in the crowd let off a hectic stream of vituperations: he turned and saw the minister standing behind him.

"I beg your pardon, minister," he said: "I didna ken that you were there."

Gordon patted him on the shoulder.

"Carry on, my man," he said: "you are expressing my feelings in a perfect fashion."

Gordon was an honest man (and incidentally a man whose kindness helped me greatly during an unhappy period of my life). It isn't the language that matters, it is the emotion behind the language, and when a minister foozles at golf it is unimportant whether he says "Bother!" or . . . alas, publishing and printing etiquette has not advanced far enough to allow me to write what I could write. A man may control his language but he cannot control his emotions or his thoughts, so that it is possible for a saint to curse like a bargee, while a sinner may be experiencing pornographic emotions during his prayers. Hence I know I am right in saying that swearing does not matter a jot in itself, but it does matter that swearing is too often the external symptom of a rotten sex education. To punish a child for swearing proves that you have got an obscene interest in sex yourself.

In schools swearing is considered one of the worst crimes. Some time ago I had an epidemic of swearing in my school. I announced that I also was interested in swearing and would hold a swearing class twice a week. There was a big turn out when my first lessons began. I gave out paper and pencils.

"We'll all write out all the swear words we know," I said. My list beat all other lists.

"Now let's try and see who can make the most obscene drawing," I said cheerfully. My drawing wasn't the best.

Then the class began to get bored.

"I'm fed up," said a boy and he walked out. The others followed. When I came to give my second lesson three days later not a soul turned up. I asked why. "Too dull," was the answer and, of course, it was too dull. When you approve of swearing and obscene drawing there is no fun in them. I hasten to add that my motive in having the class was not to suppress the outburst: I was in fact disappointed at its short duration for I had lots of interesting lessons to give. This little experience suggests that by discouraging swearing the moralists have always succeeded in making it valuable and attractive. This is another, if clumsy way, of stating that to the pure all things are impure.

The chief end of Puritanism is to suppress the pleasure-giving emotions, and its chief effect is to make those good emotions clandestinely pornographic. In Scotland, where Puritanism was extreme, sex became a vile thing. Worse still it became an unmentionable thing. Our schools which tutored the little savage in school subjects, carefully shunned the most important subject in the world. I grant that English schools are equally guilty in this respect, and that English Puritanism has much to answer for. Yet I believe that there is more sex repression in the Scottish home than in the English. Consider the modern cult of nakedness. There are many families in the south which give their children no complexes about nakedness: father and mother do not try to hide their bodies from their children. There are very few Scots families in which a son or daughter has seen the parents naked. There are remarkably few Scots parents who tell their children the truth about birth. The one good factor in the Scots fear of sex is that children up north have on the whole a less virulent guilty conscience about masturbation: the shy parents fear to mention so dreadful a thing to their offspring, and thus they avoid the appalling consequences of telling dangerous lies that make children miserable for life. Unfortunately, however, the moral atmosphere of kirk and school and home have an effect on the child that is almost as dangerous as the direct lie about the evils of masturbation.

The moral suppression is applied just as much to natural functions as to sex. I think it was only recently that my native town of Forfar instituted a public lavatory for women. Women in Scotland were evidently supposed to be above such ordinary vulgar things as lavatories.

You can sum up the morals of a country fairly accurately by studying the various expressions that cover the term Going to the Lavatory. In France and Germany, indeed in most European countries, a lavatory is a lavatory, but in Scotland you never go to the lavatory: you go to wash your hands, or to see a man about a dog. Puritanism is a master of evasion, but still interest will out: on two occasions I have heard women describe a Writer to the Signet as a W.C.

My opinions on Scotland and the Scots are not of much importance. But as a teacher of some experience my opinions on sex education of children should be of some importance. A child should be taught about sex all the way up. It should have its every question answered truthfully and sincerely, yes, and unmorally. It should never be corrected for interest in its own sex organs or in its excrement. Nothing should be said or done that will give the child a guilt feeling about its body. If all children were brought up freely about sex the world would be freed from the neurotic unhappy people who hate life and themselves.

How then can a Scotland that has been brought up evilly in sex matters have a creative value in education? What does it matter if you pass your Higher Leavings when your soul is warped by sex repression? Sex is no more sacred than cheese: one part of the body is as good as another. Sex is an instinct that should be free to express itself, and by expressing itself I do not mean being a Don Juan or a prostitute or for that matter a respectable married person. I mean that if sex is looked upon as a natural pleasant thing that has its place, its honest open place in life, then we have a people that is healthy and kind. Sex repressions always militate against kindness: the most venomous gossip is always the sexually starved old woman . . . of either sex.

That the Scots are kind is most wonderful. They are kind in spite of their warped sex repression. All the suppressions of all the puritan killjoys from John Knox onwards have not succeeded in killing the essential love of life that is in the lowland Scot. But it would be of value to know where in Scotland whisky was most popular. For whisky and sex repression gang thegither. Whisky enables one to escape for a time from a world that has moral principles. In more southern countries where sex is not so suppressed drunkenness is seldom seen . . . not that it is seen so very much in the north: we carry our liquor pretty well, we Scots.

Have you ever wondered why whisky is called a Drop o' the Auld Kirk? It certainly cannot be that whisky and the Auld Kirk arouse the same emotions: rather is it likely to be that the Auld Kirk had the best appreciation of the dram, for God knows, the

Auld Kirk had good reason to escape from its own reality. Burns was quite wrong when he said that whisky and freedom gang thegither. When you are free in soul you don't require the warming illusion that comes from whisky. Luckily I, for one, am not free enough of soul to despise utterly the merits of the contenting nip, but I am glad that I haven't been drunk in the last twenty-five years. Whisky is a good servant at night but a bad master next morning.

In a country like Bavaria, where much beer is drunk, a merry evening tends to gravitate towards song and dance. In Scotland a binge often ends in argument and sententiousness. In the first stage of a good soak the Scot is happy, but, later on, he loses this happiness, and picks bones with people, that is, he becomes a moralist again. No man will argue unless he is a moralist, and further, the man who knows about a subject will not argue about it. We argue to convince ourselves, and the Scot has a michty job to convince himself, for even in his cups he keeps assuring the world that he isn't drunk . . . which means that he knows he is.

Here a friend has looked over my shoulder and asked: " Is this a book on education or on Johnny Walker? " I appreciate the justice of his question,

EDUCATION AND SEX

but I know that I am not really interested in education. In fact I don't know what education is, although I know what it isn't. You cannot write about education and think only of schools. "An educated man is a man who has forgotten all that he learned in school." Very near the truth this. Schools do not make a nation: the nation makes its schools. The adults give to the children what they think children ought to have, and I have the suspicion that the Scots use school subjects in the way that the English Public Schools use sport—as a means of distracting attention from the devil. The complete absence of emotion from the curriculum confirms this suspicion. The emphasis on head work and the neglect of handwork is symbolic, for thinking is safer than doing. Moreover in symbolism the head is spiritual while the body is earthly. Homer Lane used to say that a clergyman buttons his collar at the back, so that when he looks in the glass he believes that he has made a complete separation between the spiritual and the earthly. It was Lane's joke, but there is truth in it, as there is in every joke. The earthly body means sexuality, and the school subject, so much valued in Scotland, was, and is, a defence against sexuality, sexuality in its broad sense of earthly and physical pleasure. The discipline of the school has the same object—to restrain youth, to castrate it, although there are other motives. Scotland is notorious for its use of the tawse, and the villager often greets a child returning from school with the cheerful query: "Weel, Wullie, did ye get yer licks the day?" Corporal punishment is now known to be actuated largely by sex repressions: it is the punishment of the hated hand . . . in the other fellow, and everyone who has studied psychology knows why the hand is an object of hatred. In southern schools, where homosexuality is an object of repression, punishment naturally gravitates to caning of the posterior. I will say for Scotland that it isn't a homosexual country: its co-education system is much healthier than the English insane segregation school organization.

This tawsing business in Scotland is a national disgrace. I am always being told that I preach against evils that are long since dead, yet too often I hear of children in Scotland who are strapped for making mistakes in spelling and sums. I say that the root of the evil is sex repression. Many teachers, especially women teachers, are sex starved, and sex when it is starved will find an outlet in anxiety and hate. Married women have long been forbidden to teach, the reason given being that they should be supported by their husbands, and should not take the bread out of the single woman's mouth. That reason is a rationalization. The deep unconscious reason is that a married woman has had experience of sex, and is therefore dangerous for young children. She might be too human in her dealing with children, too emotional. Besides the evil-minded boys might make lewd guesses about her night life. A woman is not considered a danger when she is a mother at home dealing with her own children, because the fact of adult sexuality is so skilfully kept secret in the home that the children are supposed to imagine that it doesn't exist. When as a boy I learned the secret of birth, I was quite willing to believe it so long as it applied to other parents: my parents, of course, could not be like that.

So long as education is linked up with bourgeoise morality we shall have the hate element in our schools. It is the human right of all people to have a sex life, and if this can only be had through the respectability of marriage, then marriage will have to cease to be our criterion if we want to have a population that is free from the hate that sex repression produces. The intolerance of Scotland in the matter of the unmarried mother is damnable and of its father the devil . . . by the devil I mean, of course, what the Calvinist would call God. Is there a woman teacher in Scotland who would not get the sack at once if she had an illegitimate child? There isn't. But I know of more than one case in England where the woman was allowed to keep her job. Is there a minister in Scotland who would keep a servant who had a bastard? I hope there is. I know that Jesus would have increased a lassie's wages so that the child should have the best chance.

The sex morality of Scotland is cruel, as it is narrow and un-Christlike. But I fear that the same can be said about most nations: with the exception of a few primitive races, humanity has a hateful attitude to sex. Whatever the economic causes of war, the psychological cause is primarily the hate of life that the hate of sex engenders. The ugliest result Christianity has had, has been to make sex ugly and secretive. When man was primitive and had no property, sex was approved of and was not sinful, but when man began to acquire property he began to make laws to protect that property. Sex became included in the idea of property, and sex morals were invented with the aim of retaining sex for the property owners. And when man had no sense of property he had no wars, so that the suppression of sex leads naturally to the expression of the hate that is necessary for wars. We see it in the school where the punishing teacher is the sexually repressed teacher, and punishment is war—an easy war against a victim who cannot fight back. We see it in society's condemnation of sex interests that are outside the property relation of marriage. A teacher dare not be divorced: society insists on his continuing to live with the lawful wife, whom he no longer loves, or who no longer loves him. Marriage is emotionally a love arrangement and economically a property one. If the emotional element dies, as it so often must, the property and respectable element is compelled to remain by public morality. But, obviously, a marriage without the emotional factor is an evil one. If St Paul was right in holding that it is better to marry than to burn, it is right to say that it is better to be divorced than to live in hell. An unhappy marriage is the worst evil in child life, and a warring father and mother will give a child fears and hates that fashion his life history. Any moral code that makes sex a matter of respectability and duty is a code that must in its ultimate effects promote unhappiness among children. When the parent is unhappy the child is unhappy. What I write now applies equally to England, only in the south there is a growing tendency to a saner morality among the intelligentsia. True the B.B.C. is said to sack any employee who has been divorced, but then the B.B.C. has most of the faults and few of the merits of a Calvinist Session House. It looks as if each programme were drawn up with the motive of pleasing the Men of Harlech . . . and Dornoch. It is sad that we haven't a Rab Burns who would give us a sequel to *Holy Willie's Prayer* in the form of an *Ode to Broadcasting House*. Like the schools and kirks the B.B.C. refuses to give any information on any subject that matters, which being interpreted means that it is respectable and safety-firstish. Instead of being a helpful and releasing force, the B.B.C. preserves the *status quo* in morals and economics, and its influence in a repressed country like Scotland cannot be a good one. It is on the side of Knox, and when Burns makes a slip in a variety turn the puritanical and sanctimonious feathers fly, for the B.B.C. is the guardian of family life and morals.

I wish our moralists would do a little wondering why the music-halls are full while the kirks are empty, why *The News of the World* has the largest circulation among Sunday papers. The music-hall deals with life and sex in a broad way, and *The News of the World* publishes stories of life and sex and crime that interests the emotional side of men. I often say that this paper is the best text-book on psychology in the world, and I think that it deserves its success. There is an Elizabethan healthiness about it that is like a bracing wind. Ibsen was right in saying that the majority is always wrong. It is—in rational matters, but, in the irrational matters that belong to the instincts, the majority is always right. Scotland, like other Christianized lands, is ruled by its emotional minority. Its sex morality is determined by its consciously sexless but unconsciously oversexed Bumbles. Only a pervert will insist on spreading his notions of sex morality . . . if they are repressive notions. The spiritual in life is the creative in life, yet Puritanism has identified spirituality with deadly possession and destruction of all that is finest in humanity. Spirituality allied itself with property, and, all down the line of its history, the kirk has moralized to the poor while winking at the vices of the rich. Even that selfless body of enthusiasts, the Salvation Army, accepts the donations of the robbing rich, donations given gladly because the Salvation Army, by concentrating on the individual sinner, helps to keep the poor from facing the much more important fact of the national sin that divides men into exploiter and exploited. So the Salvation Army of the bourgeoisie, The Oxford Group, with its bunk about "hurting Jesus" when you say a bad word like "Skunk" (*vide* a book called *Inspired Children* by one of them), and its impious "guidance" even in the matter of choosing a hat, fits in neatly with the other advances toward Fascism—the last stand of possessive capitalism.

I am sorry that I cannot confine my text to Scotland. Scotland is a province of capitalism and the morality that capitalism demands. I fear that it is waking up to the evils of capitalism less quickly than some other countries are doing. In Scotland we have an intelligent and forceful proletariat, but it is a subservient proletariat. Why? It may be because of the strong Irish element in such places as Clydeside and Dundee, an element that is directed by the priesthood, the priesthood that serves its Lord and Master . . . property. It may also be, to some extent, that the fiery Highland Scot remains outside of industrialism, and serves humbly his southern laird. However it is, the fact remains that the proletariat of Scotland is too passive outside the gates of a futba' match.

EDUCATION AND SEX

Scotland's passion for football may have something to do with her sex repression, for football, like most games, has much sexual symbolism in it, both homosexual and heterosexual. An enthusiasm for football is always a sign of degeneration in a race: it is an uncreative interest, for only twenty-two men play while thousands look on. At this moment the first news of Italy's gangster attack on Abyssinia has come through, but I could bet that in Scotland tonight the average man will read the football results before he reads the news of this criminal war. Football must be an excellent defence for the people who possess. Thousands of semi-starved workers give an enthusiasm to football that might well be used in the building of a new and better Scotland. Sport is the refuge of the uncreative: it sidetracks the libido of life. The stout man, who does his round of gowf once a week, can claim that his game is in part medicinal, but the spectator at a football match can make no claim at all except the lame one that he likes to watch clever play. The last football match I saw was in Dundee many years ago. My only recollection of it is that half the crowd seemed maniacal about shouting to the home team to kick " the bastards in the heid." So much for the homosexual element. The only psychically healthy men at a football match are the players and possibly the referee, although by the end of some matches he is decidedly unhealthy. Professionalism in any sport denotes a race that is going downhill; the professionals may be and are excellent players, but it is the tendency to look on as a spectator that spells deterioration. For if you look on at games you will be likely to look on at life. Lookers on see most of the game, but it does not help them for they never learn to play.

The games tradition of the English Public School and the football tradition of Scotland are similar in this, that both denote a false education. The creative faculty in Public Schools has little if any outlet unless in the inferior form of play. There are two kinds of play; the spontaneous play of childhood with its phantasy, and the organized conscious play of the adolescent and adult. The former is suppressed by desks and schoolbooks, while the latter is encouraged because "it cultivates the team spirit." I am not contending that, if not encouraged, older children will not play organized games. In my school, where nothing is compulsory, we have very good hockey and tennis teams, organized by the pupils themselves, but there are individual pupils who never play games, preferring to do their play in creative form, working in brass or tinkering with motor-cycles. What I object to is the encouragement of organized games in the form of the worship that takes place in the Public Schools by compulsion, and in the Scottish football grounds by the compulsion that comes from an uncreative education. Creation and sex are alike: when creation is free, sex is free, and vice versa. Football fanism is allied to Scotland's repressed sex. This fits in with Reich's theory, as quoted above, for it is the downtrodden, suppressed working-class that turns its warped sex to football. Ah, but doesn't Russia play football? It does, but it built a new civilization and then put up its goal posts: Scotland stares at its goal posts and does nothing to wipe out the blot on civilization made by the industrialism of Dundee and the Clyde. Castrated by Calvinism or by Capitalism? By both: they work well together.

VII

SCOTS HUMOUR AND EDUCATION

SCOTLAND has a distinctive sense of humour. Like most humour it is masochistic in substance, yet the humour of Scotland is almost too masochistic: like Jewish humour it laughs at the race, and, like the Jews, the Scots are a downtrodden race. The Aberdeen gangster who took his victim " for a walk " surely sprang from a Scots story-maker, just as the Jewish fire-raising joke sprang from a Hebrew. The ability in a man or in a nation to laugh at self is a healthy one . . . when the laughing at self isn't done to forestall the other fellow's invention of the joke.

Sense of humour is of great value, of much greater value than sense of mathematics or of religion. Every child should have its sense of humour cultivated, and, if humour had its place in the curriculum, humanity would not tolerate such things as tall hats, evening dress (male), mourning clothes, clergyman's dress, dignity, respectability. Scotland keeps her humour out of her schools and her universities. True the teacher and the professor occasionally make a joke, but humour, like sex and tobacco, is the prerogative of the grown-up. I once tried to be jocular in an essay at the university: my professor warned me against repeating the offence. The child in school must keep his sense of humour to himself. Humour, like laughter, is a cleansing thing, and when you have a solemn thing like a school or a kirk, humour is dangerous. There is no humour in religion: there is no joke in the Bible. The only minister I have heard make his congregation laugh (in public) was the parish minister of Forfar when I was a boy. There is no laughter in a kirk, and when there is laughter in a school it is too often the nasty laughter that arises from a teacher's cruel joke about a pupil. Laughter is a leveller: it makes all men one: it destroys differences in youth and age, rich and poor. For a teacher to laugh with his pupils would be to be level with them, to be human like them, to be young like them. Teachers as a class fear to be human. Some teachers will not smoke in the presence of their pupils, and few Scots teachers will be seen entering a public house. The Scots dominie is a dull devil, fearful of compromising his little respectability, alarmed at anything that might detract from his

SCOTS HUMOUR AND EDUCATION

petty dignity. Teachers down south are a dull lot too, but in England custom allows the teacher some latitude in behaviour. It isn't a social error for a teacher or a woman to enter a bar, or to sing a comic song. The dignity of the Scots teacher would be something to laugh at if it were not so disastrous to child nature. Dignity drives humour underground, and I wonder how much the vogue of the schoolboy dirty story is due to the suppression of humour in the school.

It can be said, of course, that English or German or Chinese teachers have dignity, that they suppress humour. In all probability they do. My point is that Scotland is different. Humour, national humour in Scotland, is a gift from the gods. It is a distinctive humour with its pawkiness and solemnity and dryness. I know of no country in the world that could give us a story like the story of the Forfar-Arbroath line.

The train is just drawing out of Forfar station when a farmer eyes a young Englishman in the compartment. After a time the farmer says: " Imphm, ye'll be gaein' to Arbroath? "

" No," says the youth, " I am not going to Arbroath."

A pause.

" Ye'll maybe be gaein' to Guthrie? "

SCOTS HUMOUR AND EDUCATION

"No, I'm not going to Guthrie."

A longer pause.

"Oh, ay, imphm, ay, ye'll be gaein' to Clocksbriggs?"

"No, I'm not going to Clocksbriggs."

The farmer wipes his mouth with the back of his hand, leans forward, and says testily: "And do ye think I care a dawm *whaur* ye're gaein'?"

That is Scots humour as the Scot sees it. I now give a story of the Scot as the Englishman sees him.

An American millionaire is very ill in London. He must have a blood transfusion. Macintosh volunteers. The transfusion is a success and the hospital gives Mac a cheque for two guineas. A week later Mac has a grateful letter from the patient enclosing a cheque for a hundred pounds. Soon the millionaire relapses, and another transfusion is necessary. When sufficiently recovered, the American sends Mac a cheque for fifty pounds. Later a third transfusion is needed, and this time Mac receives nothing from the millionaire.

That should be the end of the story, but the Englishman generally needs the explanation . . . viz., that before the first operation the millionaire was a hundred per cent Amurrican in blood and then. . . .

This story isn't really a Scots story at all. It is

simply a new and clever way of drawing attention to the time-honoured Scottish meanness. Not long ago I was asked to tell a company of Englishmen some Scots stories. My best ones were hardly understood, but when I told one or two about meanness and canniness the laughter was loud. But to laugh at the Aberdonian who said on his daughter Maggie's wedding day: " Aw doot we'll have to buy new confetti, cos it was rainin' at Lizzie's weddin' " is not to grasp the humour of Scotland.

I fear that Scotland has accepted the English standard of Scots humour. Most Scots stories could just as well be told about Jews, for they mostly deal with incidents like Mactavish's seeking the boot-and-shoe department in Woolworths. The joke has worn thin, but it has been accepted by Scotland because of Scotland's masochistic inferiority complex. To be a fool is one way of getting notice, if not superiority. Individual Scots do not mind jokes about meanness, because they know they are not mean, but the nation accepts mean jokes because it feels inferior. It is of interest that a nation of secondary schools and universities should have world-wide fame as a nation that spends its time filling its fountain pens with post-office ink. A German monthly magazine had an article with illustrations on Scots meanness . . . one picture was that of the Scots taxi accident in which twenty-four people were injured. And recently a Russian friend began to tell me tales of the canny Scot. Personally I don't mind one bit, but as a patriot I dislike the spirit of a nation that allows the world to make one of its greatest assets a traveller's tale. For Scots humour is a great asset. Better than any other country could Scotland have founded a Chair of Humour in Edinburgh University . . . and a damn sight more good it would have done than a Chair of Greek or Moral Philosophy. Humour *is* philosophy. It is emotional and often a corrective to intellectualism. The exquisite humour of Barrie's woman, who hadn't been invited to the " layin' oot " of a relative's corpse, is worth all his mystically sentimental dramas—and worth a great deal more than most of the heavy books written—say—about Scots education or religion. The Scot intellectualises too easily. That is why the Leaving Certificate and the M.A. degree are taken so easily in his stride. He represses his emotion, and in doing so, represses much of his innate humour. The joke about a Scot's taking a week to see the point of a story has some foundation in fact: he seeks to find something more esoteric than the obvious point, that is, he treats his jokes as he treats his sermons . . . he *thinks* about them. But, speaking generally, the joke you have to think over is a bad one. Laughter and thought are very ill-mated companions.

Education in Scotland is primarily concerned with thought—thought about the things that matter least in life. A good guffaw might blow the whole educational system sky-high. It all comes back to the vexed question of religion. To laugh is to be on the devil's side, and our Scots education is only the modern variant of Calvinism. Thought about heaven has degenerated into thought about mathematics or history: fear of hell has become fear of social failure. God has become Capitalism, the devil Communism. The devil is a merry soul with a ringing laugh of hope, and laughter is always suspect because of its satanic founder. By laughing at its alleged meanness Scotland is evading the issue. It should laugh at its heavy-footed respectability and dignity and exams. and kirks and Sabbath. But, if it did, it might have to set fire to its schools and kirks.

VIII

EDINBURGH AND ST ANDREWS

I HAVE never in my travels seen a more beautiful town than Edinburgh, nor a more charming town than St Andrews. I want to write about them, but I grant that my impressions of them come from the years 1900 to 1912.

St Andrews, the City by the Sea, deserves immortality as the scene of the foundation of the Royal and Ancient Golf Club. As a seat of learning it does not deserve immortality. That its university has turned out some fine scholars and men of action no one will doubt, but scholarship is a little thing. St Andrews is a small provincial town and only nominally a city. Its university is situated in its centre, and it cannot escape the influence of the narrowness outside its doors. In 1908 I hesitated as to whether I should go to St Andrews or Edinburgh. I chose Edinburgh because I fancied that the life in Edinburgh would be less narrow than the life in St Andrews. And I think that I should make the same choice again, although the life at Edinburgh University can be narrow enough.

St Andrews is a terrible mother. It is an all-embracing octopus from whose arms the student never wholly frees himself. I have never met a St Andrews student who did not have a backward emotional longing for the romance of St Andrews. And its romance is strong. I feel a thrill when I look along Market Street and see the red-gowned students against the grey beauty of the cathedral ruins. I can sit beside the Castle and see its historical pageant pass before me. When lately I visited Edwin and Willa Muir in St Andrews I was frankly envious of their being able to live in a house that overlooked the Castle. I love St Andrews and I fear it. It drags one back to the glory that was, and in doing so prevents one from seeing the glory that will be. It is indeed an Alma Mater . . . but an Alma Mater becomes terrible when she will not allow us to cut the apron strings.

St Andrews University is possibly the least cosmopolitan university in Scotland. If it is true, and I believe it is, that the best education a university affords is the rubbing up against other men, then St Andrews has a great handicap. Its students are mostly men and women from the neighbouring counties, from towns like Perth and Forfar and Dundee and Cupar. It is not very helpful to rub up against Perth men if your native town is Stirling. I should imagine that Aberdeen University suffers from a similar provincialism.

St Andrews is a happy university: it is because of its happiness that its students look backward as if to Paradise. Symbolically it is childhood, an ideal childhood when one was free. Most of its students have come straight from home and school, and the delights of the free life in digs, and the social life in the university, attach the emotions to St Andrews for ever. If Scottish home and school life were not so deadly dull, I think that St Andrews would lose much of its regressive pull.

About the work done in St Andrews University I have little to say. It is no better and no worse than the work done in Edinburgh or Oxford or Yale. A university education is a school education on promotion. It is mostly concerned with what is dead—dead languages, dead philosophies, dead histories, dead religions. How alive its science is I have no means of knowing, but I know that in any university a science (or art) like psychology is far behind modern needs and beliefs. The life of a university is in its students, not its professors and their subjects. And St Andrews students, though very much alive, are alive in an adolescent way. It is little wonder that they look back sadly to their joyous life at college, when they have graduated into weary ministers and teachers and solicitors. St Andrews is glad because the rest of Scotland is so dreadfully dull.

Edinburgh University is a different proposition. I was there for four years, and, since leaving it, I have had no desire to see it again, and no wish to hear what is going on there. I love St Andrews but I am indifferent to Edinburgh. How much of this lack of love for Edinburgh is due to personal difficulties I cannot say. As a student I had a hard four years, lunching daily on threepence, and chalking my one dress shirt when I got press tickets for the opera. Yet I wonder if anyone can love Edinburgh. Its beauty is a cold beauty: its folk are a frigid folk: to me the only warm places in Edinburgh are the Cowgate and the Canongate. To live in Murrayfield would break my heart.

Edinburgh is too large to be comfortable, and too small to be cultural. It has always been a mystery to me how the people live. There are a few publishing companies, a few breweries and . . . no, I must look up an encyclopædia. . . . " A professional rather than a manufacturing town, in printing, publishing, bookbinding, insurance, banking and retail shop-keeping, Edinburgh claims to be second to London: other industries include brewing, distilling, milling, baking, rubber-works, engineering, chemicals, scientific instruments, paper-making, fisheries. Education is called Edinburgh's 'chief industry'; one of the greatest educational centres in the world . . ." then a list of its educational establishments (*The New Age Encyclopædia*).

That spoils my theory that the well-dressed paraders of Princes Street live by taking in each other's washing. The description might have included the big number of lawyers in Edinburgh. It may be the influence of the professional people that has preserved one or two theatres in Edinburgh, just as it must have been the uncultural commercialism of Dundee that made that city close the one theatre it had.

Edinburgh is Princes Street and the Cowgate, and the North Bridge does not span the gulf between. . . . It is a town of acute snobbery, the snobbery of a class that is not sure of itself. It is an unfriendly town. I can only guess that it is the east wind that makes Edinburgh folk so unfriendly. Glasgow folk have the gift of making you feel they love you, even if you are only asking the way to Buchanan Street, but I always approach an Edinburgh man with a little timidity. No, it cannot be the east wind, for Dundee folks are as obliging as Glasgow folks. What is it then that makes Edinburgh so suspiciously unfriendly? Not its proletarians in the Cowgate: they are always friendly. It is Princes Street and all that it stands for that colours Edinburgh with its icy personality. Years ago, when I edited the university magazine, I had an editorial entitled " The Peril and the Pity of the Princes Street Parade." I am sure that the title was the best of the editorial. I have a vague recollection of advocating the use of cap and gown as a means of escaping from the necessity of snobbishly dressing up to the Princes Street standard. The editorial possibly followed a visit to St Andrews, where cap and gown did lend a distinction that had nothing to do with money. But the youthful tirade against Princes Street holds some truth today. Princes Street with its luxury shops and its moneyed customers is the most influential factor in Edinburgh. Princes Street brings snobbery from its home in the suburbs into the centre of the city. The tastes of Edinburgh are Princes Street tastes, that is, class tastes. In my student days it was bad form to smoke a pipe in Princes Street between 10 a.m. and 1 p.m. Bond Street never was as bad as that. Edinburgh attaches importance to outer things. I may be wrong, but I have the impression that on any fine morning you wouldn't find two people in Princes Street who had any ideas on—say—psychology or Communism or the modern drama, but I had the same idea the other day when at Newmarket I attended my first race meeting (by accident). Edinburgh strikes me as a typical middle-class town with a cheap Kultur . . . and I admit that that may only be my class prejudice.

Edinburgh University is not Edinburgh. It is to some degree cosmopolitan. It has many students from the colonies and a fair proportion of coloured students . . . who, in my day, were usually called damned niggers because of the colonial students' influence. It has a professoriate that keeps to itself. In my four years I never met a professor or a lecturer socially. The majority of the students are poor, their fees, as mine were, are paid by the Carnegie Trust. They live in humble digs, and many of them attend their classes and return to their digs, without having any social intercourse at all. The well-to-do students, most of them medicals, have some social life in their

Union. In my time there were various Students' Societies, but only a small minority joined these. It was a life without a centre. Even your professors did not know you. I recall an incident when Professor Chrystal died. I was editing *The Student*. I went to see Professor Saintsbury. I told him that I should be grateful if he would write an appreciation of Chrystal for the magazine.

"As a matter of fact," he said in his high shrill voice, "I am just going into my Honours Class, and I intend to say something about Professor Chrystal there. If you are quick at taking notes you can come in."

"That's all right," I said, "I have been in your Honours Class for two years."

He looked at me in surprise.

"Really! What's your name?"

"Neill."

"Oh, yes, quite so." He studied me through his glasses. "Dear me, how you've grown!"

I had been six foot high for ten years before that.

George Saintsbury may have been more indifferent to his students than other professors, but I can safely say that not one of them knew me by name or sight.

Years later I spent a week end in Oxford, and on

the Sunday morning I was invited to take part in a debate on Macdougall's psychology at eight in the morning. In Edinburgh I was never invited to debate anything at any hour. One felt that one was in a great machine and not even a cog in that machine. It was a most impersonal university.

What merits the teaching side had I do not know. I sat through Professor Macgregor's course in Natural Philosophy without understanding a word of what he was talking about. Professor Walker's Chemistry was more interesting, but I felt that he was wasting his time, because his little text-book gave us all the information that we needed. Professor Lodge (later Sir Richard) lectured on History. I enjoyed his lectures very much, but here again his books could have given us all that he gave us. Like Saintsbury, he was a stranger, taking no interest in us as individuals. I think he knew my name for a week because he threw me out of the class one day, mistaking me for a cheery bloke behind me who was an adept at cat-calling.

So far as the professors were concerned a university education in Edinburgh was negative. We did not listen to what they said, because we knew we could get it all from their books. I sat and drew sketches and wrote letters for two years in George Saintsbury's classes. I feel sure that George wouldn't have cared.

The lecture system is an anachronism. I believe it dates from the time before the invention of printing. It is a waste of professorial and studental time. Think of Walker having to waste his time teaching raw students the elements of chemistry, when in a sensible State he would be allowed to do research all day long. Think of Saintsbury having to dilate on Dryden to a crowd of students who were not listening. It was Barrie who described a lecture by Chrystal as a confidential conversation with his medallist. I think that our professors hated the sight of us, and did so rightly. Only an inferior can teach.

The English way of having dons and small classes must be much better. A small group allows some outlet for emotion. I think of the History Class in Edinburgh, a large packed lecture room in which the only emotion one could express was the anti-professor one of drumming with the feet or whistling with the fingers.

I realize now what I am trying to say in these pages: to say that emotion is necessary in all education. That unless education appeals to the instincts it is false and superficial. Edinburgh University left my

EDINBURGH AND ST ANDREWS

emotions to themselves. The curriculum was purely intellectual and uncreative. I spent my time studying English Literature from Beowulf to Pater without having to exercise any more creation than is required for an essay.

Kultur in a broad sense there was none. An occasional Rectorial Election with its fun and almost complete absence of political perception. A few afternoon concerts in the Union. Rugger matches for those who liked them. Otherwise the life was barren and narrow. To say that Edinburgh is a great educational centre is just not true. A learning shop if you will: a factory for mass production of degrees. But I found it possible to take a degree there and go out into a world that showed me how badly educated I was. Nine years after graduating I went to live in Dresden, having there a position that brought me into contact with the Kultur of Central Europe. The maid who swept my room talked to me of *The Ring* and *The Rosenkavalier*. Her young man made hammered brass ornaments that were fine art. Painters talked of their work: I listened to musicians discussing the then new Bela Bartok compositions. I discovered the vast territory of dancing and plastic art. And I met people with new ideas and a new

Weltanschauung. That today the anti-Kultur of Hitlerism has suppressed most of what was of value in Germany is not to the point. The point is that a provincial town like Dresden, a town much about the same size as Edinburgh, had something to give that Edinburgh had not given me. Geographical factors naturally had much to do with it. Dresden is within easy reach of Berlin, Munich, Prague, Vienna, Budapest. It was in Dresden that the first performance of *Der Rosenkavalier* was given. Edinburgh is geographically at the back of beyond. The only centre that can give it Kultur is London . . . and the Kultur of London is so uncertain that I, for one, dare not face the unpleasantness of going to a play in any of its commercial theatres. The lack of Kultur in Britain can be seen in the jewellery shop windows. I have often walked along Princes Street and down Bond Street without seeing a single article of jewellery that struck me as being of artistic value, whereas one of the minor joys of my life is to see the artistic metal work of Brussels or Copenhagen or Vienna.

But there is the vexed question as to what is Kultur. It is like charm: you cannot define charm but you cannot mistake it. I have considered the suggestion that Kultur means admiration of the foreigner's goods as a means of disparaging what is at home. There is often an element of this in the rhapsodizing about foreign Kultur. I have tried to discover such a motive in myself, and have found some satisfaction in the thought that, because a thing is foreign, I do not necessarily like it. The scholastic system of Europe is hellish and I dislike it: I dislike the manners of Germans in railway carriages: I dislike the arrogant attitude that Swedish men have to their wives and families: I dislike the Berlin policeman. There are many things in Britain that appear to be much better than their equivalents on the Continent. But there are many things also that are worse. English beer, English cooking, English coffee, the English Sunday are in my opinion bad, while any continental tobacco or tea is execrable. German manners with their stiffness are not to be compared with our freer ways of intercourse.

But these are small things. In many of the bigger things in life our insular life is lacking much that the Continent has. We have no opera; most of our plays are tripe; few of our films reach the standard of the German, French, and Russian films. Our newspaper headline news that is of no consequence. I have never seen a continental paper that would give a cross headline to a topic like " Body Found in

Mayfair Dustbin." (I hasten to add that I have never seen such a headline in *The Scotsman* or *The Glasgow Herald* either.)

There are ways in which Scotland compares most favourably with Germany. We have not the arrogance of Prussianism: we do not behave in a barbaric way to Jews: we have not that slave mentality that makes militarism a walk-over for the bosses and sadists. We have, as yet, no concentration camps and no Reichstag Fire frame-ups. Our Scottish universities are just as good as the German universities, and our schools are better than German schools. Our Scottish teachers have not the fatuity of the German teachers, who aim at uplift all the time, and a Scottish schoolboy has too much sense of humour to talk about his inner urges. Our students are a cut above the puerilities of the German universities with their infantile clubs and adolescent duels and petty dignities. I never hear from a Scots radio station voices that sound so full of hate as the voices of the Nazi leaders.

But the fact remains that in Berlin or Munich or Dresden there is the opportunity of finding what Edinburgh or Glasgow do not provide. And travellers who know tell me that the Kultur of Russia is far ahead of anything to be found in Central Europe.

EDINBURGH AND ST ANDREWS

Film critics who have been to Moscow come back to London with a deep depression at the prospect of having to write up the poorer productions of Elstree and Hollywood. Dramatic critics say that there is nothing in the world to touch the Moscow theatre. The science of Russia is far more advanced than the science of any other country. But it is not fair to compare a country that makes things for use with a country that makes things for profit. Therefore let me stick to my comparison between Edinburgh and—say—Munich.

I am now speaking about intangible things. To say that Munich has a better drama than Edinburgh is not of the highest importance. But there is in the atmosphere of Munich something intangible that makes the town a place of interest, while, after you have looked at the beauty of Edinburgh, you feel you are in a town that is not quite alive.

You can meet people with brains in Edinburgh: you can mingle with hard-headed lawyers and business men: you can flirt with pretty women. But when you leave Edinburgh you do not look back regretfully and wistfully. There is no warmth about the city: it is as hard as its Castle Rock. I speak, as I say, of intangible things. Glasgow has some warmth; so has Dundee, but Aberdeen has Edinburgh's chill.

EDINBURGH AND ST ANDREWS

Edinburgh has an ancient air of self-satisfaction and self-sufficiency. It is Tory in all senses: it is as austere as its daily *Scotsman*.

I wonder if our feelings about cities are entirely subjective. To me Vienna is warmer than Berlin, Munich than Dresden, Copenhagen than Stockholm. I wonder if my feelings, or shall I say lack of feelings, for Edinburgh is entirely due to my lonely student days, or possibly more so to the days when as a lad of fourteen I went to Buccleuch Street as a clerk in a gas meter factory, spending months of painful homesickness there.

No, the whole truth does not lie in the subjective. The dull reactionism of Edinburgh University, for example, is an objective reality. The mincing mediocrity of Murrayfield is a dull reality. Edinburgh is content to accept civilization as it is, because its people know that in another civilization its wealth and indifference would be useless. Such a city can only be termed a seat of learning if we postulate that learning is valueless. When at last civilization sweeps away the gross criminality of our capitalist world, I fear that Edinburgh will be the last stronghold of die-hardism in the north, while possibly Oxford will hold out longest in the south.

IX
THE RURAL SCHOOL

THE village school in Scotland has often been highly praised, and the praise given was very often a deserved one. Many a " lad o' pairts " has sprung from a Scots village. The old Scots dominie was often a grim devil, but he was often an efficient one. In the main the country bairn had a freer life than his town contemporary. The sexes had more chance to mix in a country school, and the discipline was usually not so severe as that obtaining in town schools, where large numbers made strict discipline necessary. Moreover, the bright scholar was in touch with his teacher, and had the chance of an almost individual tuition.

A school, however, must not be judged by its bright lads and lassies. Most of the pupils in a village school leave school at about fourteen and go on the land or the railway. When I was a boy at my father's school in Kingsmuir, near Forfar, many of the girls left at fourteen and went to slave in the jute factories of Forfar, working from six to six, and trudging the

THE RURAL SCHOOL

two miles there and back in all weathers. The boys became ploughmen or roadmen or railway men. A few became apprentices to blacksmiths and joiners.

Education then was very much as it is now. Children were divided into classes according to age or brains. Subjects were, the usual Reading (from " Readers "), Arithmetic with sums on acres and pecks and poles, vulgar and decimal fractions, proportion, Writing in Copy Books (of all books the most likely to produce an intense inferiority complex, for no child could hope to rival the copperplate of the pattern lines). Geography meant maps and learning strings of rivers, names of towns and their products. To this day I have in my memory tags like " Hexham—famous for hats and gloves," " Axminster—carpets," " Dunstable—straw hats." History I cannot remember learning until I was in the ex-Sixth, when we had a text-book that told the " truth " about the Indian Mutiny and the Crimea. English meant parsing and analysis and dictation, and later the writing of a short story that had been read out to us. The most pleasing lesson was called Intelligence, where we made a semi-circle, and my father asked us the meanings of words and phrases from our Readers.

That in brief was our schooling. By making the

teacher's salary depend on his "Report" the Scotch Education Department with its Inspectors saw to it that the dominie drilled his pupils earnestly, if grimly.

What happened to a boy who left school at fourteen and went to be "loon" on a farm? Naturally he forgot his acres, roods, poles, his parsing and analysis, his geography, his sums. He set his bonnet at a rakish angle and soon mastered the art of squirting out tobacco juice from his mouth. I recall my father's Evening Classes. Each evening, when the lesson was over, the schoolroom floor was a lake of Bogey Roll saliva. Ploughmen in those days were distinctive: they wore coloured leather-collars, cheese-cutter caps, and they had a studied ploughboy walk. They took a pride in their horses and kept their harness spick and span. Their favourite noun was bugger. They were friendly, simple, carefree. They would have been very much the same if the village school had not existed. Few of them read in their bothies. On a Sunday or after working hours they would meet at The Brig and converse, but all I can remember about their conversation was a series of "Aye, man" and "Yea, man?" But they must have had their lighter moments, for it was from them that I learned the *Ball o' Kirriemair*.

THE RURAL SCHOOL

Obviously the schooling which I have described was the wrong one for a rural community. I think I first criticized it when, as a pupil teacher, I saw the chairman of the School Board okay the register with the words " Number presant, 97 ", but to say that the system did not turn out good spellers is not ground enough to condemn it. It stood condemned because of its divorce from the real life of the community. A boy left school with a knowledge of Simple Interest but he could not measure a field. He was taught nothing about botany or agriculture or biology. He had no instruction is using a hammer or a plane. I am not advocating the turning of education into a utilitarian preparation for wage-slavery. I am arguing that rural children would find interest in the simple life they and their parents lived. Schooling did not interest most of them, but practical work would have done so. I think about the pleasant hours I spent collecting birds' eggs or catching minnows. A good system would have made these hobbies a part of school life. What use was the geography of Africa to me when there was a living geographical study at the school door? I cannot recall having any ideas about the life outside the school. I was not conscious that the cattle I loved to " drove " were destined for

THE RURAL SCHOOL

slaughter. A farm was not a commercial proposition to me: it was a paradise of barns and byres. I was never conscious that the ploughmen were sweated labourers. Nor were the boys who were destined for the plough conscious of their condition. Rural education consciously aimed at producing exploitees, and I can remember occasions on which my father was impotently angry because farmers kept children away from school to gather potatoes. Later the " tattie holiday " was made for the benefit of the farmers. I suppose that the deep motive of the School Boards was to keep the children as unconscious of their surroundings as possible. If that were the motive it was highly successful: I cannot imagine a conversation about Socialism round a bothy fire: I cannot hear a foreman trying to convert the cattleman to Credit Reform: if there is such a thing as a Ploughman's Trade Union in Forfarshire I express my surprise.

The land deadens. It is difficult to be brilliant in a ploughed field. The rustics in Russia have been the last to accept Communism. It is comparatively easy to exploit country folk . . . unless you are trying to sell them something. At the same time it would be evil to try to force a foreign culture on the peasant. I don't want to see Jock develop the cocky alertness of the cockney: I should hate to see Jean tossing her head like a Mayfair chamber-maid. But more could be done for the peasants. The rural school should bring them into touch with painting and handcraft and music and dancing: it should give them self-expression in acting and singing: it should teach modern history and economics and such science as will be interesting in later life. During the summer the pupils should be out of doors all day. Roughly speaking any rural scheme should be experimental with the view to allowing children to select what interests them. It is improbable that arithmetic's charms would win against those of metal-work or pottery, that the exports of China would put the joy of dancing in the shade.

I am talking without my book. It may be that there are rural schemes in Scotland that are as far advanced as the rural scheme of East Suffolk, where I live.

Educational facilities in a country district are few for those beyond school age. In recent years women's clubs have sprung up all over the country, but these, like the Girl Guides movement, are apparently propaganda centres for the rich. The lady of the manor patronizes the local Institute, and the members sew and give concerts and listen to nice little talks by the patronesses. I should think that these clubs are of much use during election times, and I do not suppose that any of them invite Harry Pollitt to lecture to them. They appeal to the snobbery of the poor, and are milestones on the road back to feudalism. If they were spontaneous clubs springing from the communal desire for companionship they would be worthy of support and praise. Organized as they usually are by the upper class, they become suspect of ulterior motive at once. They have the same motive as the Scout movement has—to train youth to do its duty to the people who own Britain. That all such movements have much that is meritorious in them is true; when, however, the deepest motive is a selfish one (the perpetuation of rich and poor), the harm that such institutions do heavily outweighs their good. I am assuming that one of the most important aims of humanity should be to abolish both rich and poor, and hence I take the view that everything that hinders their abolition is inimical to humanity.

It is sad to think that many people cannot see that society is changing at a rapid rate. The haves see it more clearly than the have-nots, for they have a strong motive for seeing a danger that will attack them. I am neither politician nor economist, but as a layman it is fairly clear to me what is happening to society at present. We have always been ruled by the rich. Theoretically we were free to vote for the poor, but as the poor were badly educated and suppressed by poverty and social inferiority the rich managed to get themselves elected most of the time. Gradually the educational gulf between rich and poor narrowed, and the rich at once threw up the pretence of democracy and met the rising discontent of the workers by force. Fascism and Naziism are simply the present form of capitalism's retention of power. Folks say that Britain will never stand Fascism. Why shouldn't it? It has stood capitalism in its benign form for a long time, and there is little evidence that it will reject capitalism in its iron-fist form. As I write a National Government is likely to be returned next week by a large majority. This government will be a rich man's government, and if I were its leader I should at once embark on the logical policy of forming an armed alliance against Russia. It would be easy, for Germany has much desire to expand East . . . and we would rather have her expand East than re-expand in Africa. The immediate future of white civilization is clearly a tremendous battle between Capitalism and Communism. And no preaching will avert it and no preaching will cause it. It is inevitable. Whether

THE RURAL SCHOOL

we like it or no, it is a war that all the conscious longings for peace cannot ward off. It is useless to stir up class war: class war is there, mostly unconscious, slowly but surely growing into a force that will be an appalling nightmare. Statesmen cannot avert war because statesmen only mouth the power instinct of their groups. Mussolini did not make Fascism: Fascism made him, and, if he died, the movement would not be seriously handicapped. People will fight to the death for property, and so long as we have private property the world will be an armed camp. It is futile to attack individual capitalists. They are as kindly folk as you and I are. Capitalism has a crowd psychology—which is quite different from individual psychology. We see this in a national attitude to such a thing as capital punishment. No single man would accept the responsibility of hanging a criminal, yet the crowd will hang a man legally without any sense of guilt. Rich people are no better and no worse than poor people. They are as kindly and as charitable . . . in their own class. But as a crowd the property-owners have an emotion that is different from the emotion of the individuals composing that crowd. As a crowd they deliberately turn a blind eye to the evils that property-owning causes. As a crowd

THE RURAL SCHOOL

they know that you can only have a Rolls Royce at the expense of the propertyless who live on the border line of starvation, and as a crowd they will do everything to retain the *status quo*. So that the lady of the manor in a Scots village may act as an individual when she founds a Rural Institute. She may be genuinely pleased at her success in giving poor women an evening a week in which they will have pleasant and interesting social intercourse. And she will be unconscious of the fact that, as a member of her propertied crowd, she is trying to stem any rising of indignation against the rich. Possibly her attitude of patronage will be unconscious also: I do not suppose she ever thinks of the reason why she does not include the blacksmith's wife in her dinner-party list of invitations.

I sometimes wonder what would happen if I attempted to get a servant girl presented at court. Theoretically in a democracy anyone can be presented at court, but would Buckingham Palace accept the nomination of Susan Jane? If not, why not? Or again, why is a title given to a man who makes a fortune out of beer or cars and no title is offered to me? I am a more important man than a beer baron or a car manufacturer, because I am concerned in the production of vital human beings, while they are producers of mere commodities. I have as much brain power as Lord Beaverbrook: I am just as handsome as Lord Nuffield: I have as much humour as Lord Dewar. Why then am I left out of the Honours List? I am left out because I have no riches and consequently no power. In other words, in a Capitalist civilization, I do not count, and in a Capitalist system Susan Jane does not count. To count you must have a bank balance to count.

Thus I look upon the Scottish Rural Institute movement as a danger in post-school education. It helps to perpetuate what is in essentials a rotten civilization . . . a class civilization. Like the kirk, the Rural Institute tries to ameliorate the evils that are inherent in the possessive atrocity we call Capitalism: like the kirk it keeps the poor in their proper place.

Sexual repression is less in a village than in a town. This is partly because the countryside affords more opportunity for love-making, and partly because farm life makes sex an everyday natural thing. When I was a boy many a rural wedding followed the "cutting of the cake," and I have more than once seen a son dance at his parents' marriage.

Possibly because of this natural attitude to sex, the country has a higher standard of morality than the town. Promiscuity in a village is rare. The blacksmith does not seduce the wife of the cobbler, but the marital faithfulness of the farmer class is not always so confirmed. In the working class in general divorce is not frequent, not because divorce is expensive so much as because a hard-working person has no time for promiscuity. So we find much less neurosis among the poor. Neurosis is a luxury, and naturally the leisure classes enjoy it most. I hold, therefore, that the Forfarshire ploughmen who use coarse adjectives and sing *The Ball o' Kirriemair*, have a sex morality that is more primitive and more conducive to happiness than the sex morality of the aristocracy and middle-class. Promiscuity is not a sin in itself, but the middle-classes use it as a sin, attaching to it a sense of guilt, and consequently getting out of it a sense of insufficiency and unhappiness. Going back to Dr Reich's theory that Capitalism uses sex repression as a means of keeping the proletariat in its place—making it servile and symbolically castrated, I suggest that his theory applies almost better to the middle-class stratum of society than to the manual workers. The effect would be very much the same, for the middle-class is Capitalism's shock brigade: it is Capitalism's defence against the proletariat. This is clearly seen in Germany, where Capitalism conquered the workers by its alliance with the lower middle-class—the shopkeepers, officials, etc.

I must guard against giving the impression that the Scottish rustic is a paragon of behaviour. It is more disgraceful to have an illegitimate child in Letham village than in Glasgow, and I have often seen the women of a village treat a " fallen " sister in the vilest of manners. Naturally her strongest and bitterest critics were those fallen women who had got married when the child was seven months on the way. The fallen woman's crime is that she has given the show away. A Scots village likes to have its scandals slightly underground. It dearly loves a sexual scandal.

There is the illuminating story of the Highland hotel-keeper who advertised for a housekeeper. He selected a likely woman and showed her round the hotel. On the upper floor he pointed to the right.

" There are sax rooms alang there," he said, " and another five along to the left." Then he opened a door in the centre. " And this is our bedroom," he said.

The woman gasped.

" Our bedroom? " she cried. " Do you mean to say that I have to share a bedroom with you? "

The landlord scowled.

" Ay," he said doggedly, " ye have . . . do you

THE RURAL SCHOOL

think I'm going to have the village tellin' a lot o' bloody lies aboot *me*?"

I can imagine how some of the village women I know would skirl with laughter at that story. The married women especially. The promiscuity of a Scots village takes the form of projection: it assumes the disguise of a keen interest in the immorality of one's neighbours. Oh, yes, the married women dearly love to hear a choice tit-bit . . . but it is often the unmarried spinster who brings the story and tells it with a relish.

Ploughmen are just as much interested in sex gossip as their women-folk, only they see it from a different angle: to them it is something to laugh at but not to moralize about. Their sense of respectability is less: they are more objective about sex matters. I cannot remember any incident that suggested that ploughmen wouldn't associate with a " lassie that had had a bairn." On the contrary . . .

The relationship between the sexes at a village school is usually a healthy one, and the morality of a Scots village is founded on this relationship. Jock Broon has a much healthier attitude to women than any boy in an English Public School has. You do not find Jock dividing women into two classes as the

THE RURAL SCHOOL

Public School boy is likely to do. There is no prostitution in a Scots countryside. Sex is not contaminated by money, and when Jean marries, she marries the man of her choice without any ambition to gain wealth or position. At a venture I should say that proportionately there are more unhappy marriages in Arbroath than in Letham.

I do not believe that the village school on its learning side helps to make the country place a comparatively healthy one sexually. Sex, like health, is breezier and better on the land than in the towns. Sun and wind make the best cosmetic, and a curly-headed ploughman playing a melodeon is a better specimen of manhood than a lounge lizard. On the other hand, it must be admitted that the land dulls the perceptions, that a village boy has not the alertness of a cockney urchin, although, with the coming of the motor bus, our sober village children may have to develop an outer alertness if they are to live. And to counter the heaviness of the land the village school should scrap the heaviness of the school subject. In the past the village school has produced a few bright pupils and a vast number who, leaving school at fourteen, have developed neither the power to think nor the desire to move on. When one thinks that the electorate is composed mainly of adults who left school at fourteen, one is not surprised at the failure of democracy. I have found, or think I have found, that a boy is a boy until he is at least eighteen, and the probability is that, in a future less insane civilization, the school life will continue up to the age of eighteen or nineteen. That school life, however, will not deal with acres, roods, and poles and Brazilian exports: it will deal with what is scientific and creative. And in that time the Scottish village school will not aim at producing docile dozened ploughmen and tee-heeing farm lassies. For clodhopping could be made to produce something that wasn't a clod.

. . . .

Since the above was written I have had a conversation with a Scottish village dominie. I described the schools as I had known them, and I asked him in what way things have changed. This is roughly what he said:

Many rural schools now have school gardens, which are generally the property of the teachers, and a smaller percentage have woodwork rooms. The Scottish Education Department is encouraging the use of radio in schools, but Education Committees, in the interest of economy, are reluctant to supply receiving outfits.

Grammar is still taught very much as of old, and

it has an important place in the annual bursary examinations. Arithmetic has changed little. One still finds intricate vulgar and decimal fractions, and useless weights and measures. In history the pedigrees of kings and queens has given place to the social life of the people. Poems of the *Little Jim* variety are no longer seen in school books, but *The Village Blacksmith* is still a favourite.

School Readers are still in existence, although some Education Committees supply on hire Continuous Readers by Dickens, Henty, etc. Many pupils, after passing the qualifying exam. at the age of eleven or twelve, pass on to an Advanced Division School, where they remain for at least three years before going out as domestic servants or ploughmen.

The conditions of the children is much better than it used to be. One never sees a boy with curduroy breeks, nor does one often see a barefooted child. School dentists, doctors, nurses, and temperance lecturers pay periodic visits. Sport has been taken up in villages, and football teams play matches with neighbouring teams. The ability to play football or cricket is an asset to a teacher applying for a post. The Boy Scout Movement is encouraged by the Education Committees.

THE RURAL SCHOOL

Most schools have a library, and books are issued from headquarters at regular intervals. So well do the children attend school that many compulsory officers have been dispensed with. Corporal punishment is gradually dying out, although it is much resorted to in the north.

So far my dominie friend. I cheerfully grant that his picture is one of progress. In it, however, is a woeful lack of creative work. I see no original work done in poetry or drama or clay, no attempt at practical civics in the form of self-government. My friend felt, as I used to do when teaching in Scotland, that most of his time was wasted, that the village school is still too much of a place for marking time and learning rubbish, that its atmosphere does not blend with the atmosphere of the outside world of cows and markets. In short, a village school appears to be too academic, too tightly roped to headwork. And in spite of the merits of games as educational factors, Scotland may soon find that, like the English Public Schools, its " best " teachers are Rugby blues. But I cannot decide in my own mind which is more dangerous to children, a blue or a blue-stocking.

X

THE SCOTS WHO FLED

I DO not know the proportion of Scots who leave their native land and settle in England and the Colonies It must be a large one. The Union with England brought about the iniquity that Scotland looked to England for scope. Whether Ireland loses most of its best natives I have no means of knowing: all I have observed is that the Irish brogue is less often heard down south than the Scots accent. Round about my school in Suffolk there are many Scottish farmers, a few Swedes and Danes, but after nine years in the county I haven't heard of an Irish farmer. In London I accost many a Scottish bobby, but never an Irish one. By the way this matter of Scottish bobbies has a pleasant side. Recently I braked too suddenly and did a magnificent skid in Tottenham Court Road. A policeman came up looking very stern, took out his notebook and said: " Faur's yer license ? "

I grinned.

" Blairgowrie ? " I asked.

"Ye're wrang this time," he answered with a broad smile, "Coupar-Angus."

We had a pleasing chat about Coupar-Angus.

Now it isn't entirely ambition that makes the Scot go to England. There is in it the desire to be different, or possibly it is truer to say superior. Just as an English-speaking person feels superior on the Continent, so does a Scot feel superior in England. A Scots accent is a much better asset than a Public School education. English folk tell me that it inspires confidence, especially when the owner of the accent is a doctor. Why Scots doctors and cabinet ministers inspire confidence is a psychological problem that is beyond me. It suggests a peculiar brand of insanity in the Englishman.

What the Englishman thinks of the immigrant Scot does not matter so much as what the Scot thinks of his emigrants. The Scot is not fond of his emigrants. He quite rightly feels that they are deserters, renegades, climbers, that they think of themselves before they think of their country. And as I have said before in these pages the home Scots put the holidaying emigrant in his place every time . . . and quite right too. It is not true to say that the Scots who leave Scotland are the best Scots. Like myself some of them are good lads, but some are only inferiors who could not keep their end up at home. The English are easier to exploit than the Scots: if there is a sucker born every day down south, there is a baby born with a gold brick in its mouth up Aberdeen way. In any line there is a better chance of a career down south, and, since the days of Samuel Smiles, a career has been dear to the Scots heart. The colloquial " How are ye gettin' on? " means far more than the southern "How are you?" The tragedy is, of course, that getting on to a Scot very often means getting out.

There is an element of snobbery in this getting out. It is overdetermined by the Scots tradition that anything English is superior. But, although the English consider anything Scottish is something superior, they do not migrate to the north. The main reason for the urge towards the south is obviously that opportunity does not exist in the north. The streets of London have always been paved with gold.

The men who have left Scotland are apt to be sentimental. When a few cronies foregather in London town they like to speak tenderly of the Auld Brig or the Vinney Burn. They overcompensate for their disloyal flight by exaggerating the joys that once were theirs. Scots abroad excel in this. The emigrant

Scot would do anything for Scotland short of going back to live there.

Now what has education to do with this Scottish exodus? Very little. We do not colonize the world because of our schooling: we colonize it because of our character. We are a pioneering race that is not allowed to pioneer at home. Our so-called scholars stay at home: our poets and architects and artists rent flats in Hampstead: our heroes enter the kirk or the teaching profession or the law . . . heroes because their profession compels them to renounce the adventure of conquering England. Yet it is not wholly the strength of our character that makes us colonists and pioneers: it is also our weakness of character. The emigrant Scot is in a manner of speaking a *Fluchtmensch*: he flies from the depression of Scottish industrialism, from the Sabbath, from the deadness of town life. That is why the Scot cannot return for good to Scotland. Just as a Londoner would fear and hate to go to live in Ipswich, so would I fear and hate to go to live in Brechin. Scotland has been strangled by England. There is more misery of unemployment on the Clyde than on the Thames, because capital's centre is London, and capital has slowly withdrawn its bounty from the north. To

THE SCOTS WHO FLED

keep the northern capitalists and workers quiet, Capitalism will allow a *Queen Mary* to be built on the Clyde, but it is likely that the amalgamation of the railways will result in the closing down of locomotive works in places like Perth.

Dear me, this is supposed to be a book on Scottish education! Schools, universities, training colleges . . . what do they matter? They cannot control the great forces that have made Scotland what it is. No wonder that, when I was fifteen and incapable of learning anything, my father said to my mother: " We'll have to make him a teacher: it's all he's fit for." As a teacher himself he realized how inferior a position mere schooling holds. He saw his bright lads leave school for the plough and sink into dull indifference. That was in a village, but think of the emotions of a teacher in a Glasgow slum, when he pours useless facts into children who are to go out to squalor and stink. Education is fundamentally a psychological and economic question, and, in this system that spells degraded poverty, the obvious first step is to clear away the economic muckheaps.

And here again the emigrant Scot is a blackguard. He is a rat that has left the sinking ship. He has taken all that Scotland could give him, and gone off without a thank you. He is like a man who would have all his meals in a farmhouse, and would give all his work to the farmer on the neighbouring farm. And then the rats write books of criticism on Scotland. What a crowd! It is not to be wondered at that the home Scots give the foreign Scots a cool reception when they go back in alien motor-cars.

Yet, as one of the rats, I claim that we have something in our favour. We may not help much to solve Scotland's problems, but we sometimes help to solve world problems, and Scotland's problem is only a part of the world problems. True, we have colonized immediately in the interests of the evil system of Capitalism that has made Glasgow and Dundee open sores: we have written books that appeal mainly to the bourgeoisie: we have run pioneer schools mostly for the children of that bourgeoisie: we have climbed up stairs in the City and have helped rich men to grow richer. By running away from Scotland we did not run away from the system. Still we have managed to reach a larger public than Scotland could offer us, and in the main we have not sullied the name of Scot. At the same time I realize that my feeble defence resembles the defence of Charles I, that he was a bad king but a good father. I do not know how the other rats feel, but, personally, I have a guilty conscience about leaving Scotland, and I go back with a diffidence that is not quite natural to me. In my native town I fear to meet old friends, and when they ask how I am getting on I apologetically convey the impression that I am having very little success. Last summer I made a point of telling at least six old friends that the rather smart Humber Snipe I had with me was bought second-hand. At the time I thought that this was my kindly manner of showing them that they need not feel inferior in my presence, but I see now that the real motive behind my humility was shame at having left the sinking ship. I was saying in effect: " Yes, I know I ran away, but look at my reward? What is it but a second-hand car that no successful grocer in Carnoustie would think of buying?" I find, by the way, on looking at my Registration Book that the car was fourth-hand. I wish I had known this when I was up north in August.

Like all my books this is in the way of being a personal revelation. The Scot I know best is myself, and I can only guess at the psychology of other Scots by recognizing my own reactions. I am therefore trying now to reason out my motive in buying tartan ties and socks and deer-stalking "lairds'" bonnets when I go north on holiday. Pride of race? Maybe, but if I lived in Forfar I should never buy tartan ties nor gamey's hats. I know, of course, that the tartan trade is a racket, that it is like the Gretna Green marriages— a stunt for the foreigner. Edwin Muir, whose *Scottish Journey* I have just read (one of the best things he has written I think, with a literary style that makes me envious), seems to blame Scott and Queen Victoria for the tartan racket. He may be right, but I fancy that the racket would have automatically followed the exploitation of the Highlands as the profiteer's hunting ground, even if Scott and Victoria had never existed. The desire to wear a tartan may also be a form of snobbery encouraged by the English invasion of the moors, just as my double-snouted bonnet is possibly my snobbish ambition to be thought a laird . . . although, consciously, I have no wish to be a laird. I have fairly large grounds, a big house; I employ at least twenty-six people, but up to this minute I have never looked upon myself as a laird.

Again by ancestry I have the right to wear a few tartans: my father's father was William McNeill: my mother's folk were Sutherlands, Sinclairs, Gunns. By birth I am a Hielander . . . but I never wore a kilt and I never bought a tartan tie until I came to live in England. Possibly I would wear a kilt if my legs were a bittie fatter. Why, then, this regression to a tartan infancy that I never knew in childhood? I think that it has more to do with England than with Scotland. It is the Scots inferiority complex expressing itself in the desire to show the southern that I am a man from a superior race. I may be wrong, but I think that I see a similar attitude in men from other mountainous countries. The Jäger from the mountains of Bavaria walks along the Unter den Linden in Berlin in his native costume, with the feather of his velour hat fluttering, and his mountain shoes clattering. The people of lowland Saxony dress dully and they look spiritless. But I have not enough evidence to theorize about the differences between highland and lowland countries.

Maybe the explanation of my tartan weakness is home-sickness. Maybe the tartan tie is a mascot that protects the child that has gone from its mother land. For our first years determine our lives, and no matter where a Scot goes and no matter how long he lives there is in him a deep emotion that is fixed on the home of his infancy. We renegade Scots may write critically of Scotland, but when a Sassenach dares to speak against Scotland we do not even deign to answer him: we turn away with the conviction that he is a bloody fool. He usually is. Oscar Wilde told us that every man kills what he loves. It is a great truth. It is also a truth that no man can criticize well unless the object of criticism is one that he loves. If we can love Scotland without sentimentality all the better. We do Scotland an ill if we rhapsodize about the village green and the bothy fireside. No man should rhapsodize about a place unless he feels that his highest wish is to return to that place. Sentimentality is an emotion attached to a subject that does not merit that emotion, and the outland Scot is prone to sentimentalize the land he has deserted.

I once saw a returned Scot in a country pub. He was evidently happy to be with his old cronies. As the night went on, however, conversation flagged. The home-comer began to look uneasy: he was discovering that it was difficult to pick up threads with men he had not seen for years. An English commercial traveller entered.

"I've just motored from Liverpool," he said pleasantly.

My returned Scot's eyes brightened. He turned to the traveller.

"Liverpool?" he said. "Ah, I know Liverpool well. I spent two years in Liverpool, and—what's yours?"

When I left half an hour later the two were discussing the amenities of Harrow-on-the-Hill. The Scot had no sign of uneasiness or boredom. His old schoolfellows were talking about sheep.

In spite of the buried infantile emotions one cannot go back in life. One can never pick up old threads, and if our most loved friends were to return from the grave, we should welcome the entrance of a commercial traveller from Liverpool.

XI

PSYCHOLOGY IN SCOTLAND

MODERN psychology travels slowly. It took time to travel from Vienna to London, and it will be some time before it reaches Scotland. During the last two weeks I have had two letters, one from a lady in Edinburgh the other from a young man in Aberdeen, both strangers to me. Both asked the same question. . . . " I want to be psycho-analysed. Can you tell me of an analyst in Aberdeen (and Edinburgh) ? " I had to reply to both that I did not know of an analyst in Scotland. I suppose that there are a few in Edinburgh and Glasgow, but I never heard of them. I wish I had a list of analysts in Scotland, and, for that matter, in Manchester and Liverpool and a dozen English towns, for I get so many letters asking for advice.

I should think that the attitude of Scotland to psycho-analysis is rather like that of France. France has not accepted Freud, and I think that Scotland will accept Freud with much difficulty and reservation.

PSYCHOLOGY IN SCOTLAND

This is understandable in Scotland if it is an enigma in France, for the Scot likes to be hard-headed, and has an unholy dread of showing any emotion. The enigma of France is that its emotionalism did not welcome the psychology of the unconscious.

Freudianism would be met with much criticism in Scotland, because Freud was the man who said that sex governed life, and the repression of sex in Scotland is grimly potent. More probably is Scotland likely to take up the psychology of Alfred Adler who claims that power is the root of psychology. Both psychologies are dynamic, emotional. Scotland is reason-minded, practical. It likes to see patent results, and it likes to get its money worth. Here I think of a story J. B. Salmond told me in his inimitable way ... a story of getting your money's worth.

Two young ploughmen are dandering down the street on Forfar Market-day, looking at the stalls and the shogging boats and the hobby-horses. They come to a tent whose red-lettered bill announces a great attraction for tuppence. They decide to enter. They pay their tuppence, and are passed into the tent. Before them they see a curtain. The curtain is drawn aside and a young woman is seen standing with her back to a large board. A man, dressed like a dancing Russian, comes out carrying a sheaf of ugly-looking knives. He juggles with the knives for a little, having four of them in the air at one time. The ploughmen stare with open mouths.

Suddenly the man gives a wild shriek, and throws a knife towards the woman. It shivers in the timber within a quarter-inch of the woman's ear.

One ploughman turns to the other breathlessly.

" Christ, Wullie, he's missed her ! "

It is not easy to persuade such a race that psychology is of value, for psychology never appears to give its money's worth. Its effects are too remote. Nevertheless Scotland needs modern psychology badly, both Freudian and Adlerian psychology. There are quite a number of folks up north who could do with a spot of analysis. There is the tawsing teacher expressing his or her self-hate by projection: there is the set-minded lawyer who has escaped his criminality by looking for crime in the other fellow: there is the minister who cannot find peace because his night dreams are not holy: there is the town merchant who fails to reconcile his amours with his kirk eldership. And a nation that has Dundee and Glasgow must have a tremendous guilt complex, a crowd complex, that, added to the personal complex that

Calvinism gave it, must weigh most heavily on the nation's soul.

The men of Scotland may take to psychology more readily than the women. Scottish women have an aggressiveness that cannot be hid by smiles or lipstick. They have the appearance of being on the defensive all the time. And I fancy that the Scot fears his wife more than the Englishman does. In a Scottish home the mother is the dominating partner, and in this context I quote the words of a southern woman whom I took in my motoring party to the north.

"Scots mothers," she said, "seem to bind their sons to them with steel apron wires," and she instanced one or two incidents she had seen. On one occasion a mother in a restaurant in Princes Street was telling her son of thirty odd years exactly what she wanted him to eat. Another was a mother in Oban, who told her grown-up son that he was not to go out rowing in a boat. On both occasions the son accepted the maternal dictate without apparent remonstrance. I have seldom met a Scot who had not a strong mother fixation, or a Scottish daughter who had not a protesting attitude to her authoritative mother. It is the mother who makes the Scots home an uneasy place in which one has to think three times before one speaks, and in which one feels guilty about lighting a cigarette after a meal. I have known two village dominies who had to stand outside in all weathers to have a smoke, but I grant that they were exceptionally spoused.

Our bailies and elders and ministers may make a brave show of guarding outward morals, but it is the women in Scotland who guards private morals. The equality of the sexes in school, where girls have almost the same curriculum as the boys, may have some bearing on the circumstance that Scots wives wear the breeks so bravely, and who wears the breeks controls the morals. The parochialness of Scotland narrows the moral outlook considerably. The opinion of neighbours is something to be feared. The tragedy of the drunken husband is not that he disgraces himself, but that he disgraces his family in the neighbours' eyes. In provincial parts the family is a more important unit than it is in the cities. Thus a Scots mother pays more attention to her children's appearance than a southern mother does. The mothers of the Cowgate in Edinburgh or the Blackness Road in Dundee are, like all slum mothers, nearly indifferent to neighbours' opinion on the state of the children's faces and clothes. In respectable families, however, the policy is one of hush hush, and evil is minimised even in speech. Whisky is "spirits" (as a boy I had to ask for a bottle of *Aqua Vitae*): being drunk is "having a dram" or sometimes being "jolly"; being pregnant is to be "expecting" (cf. the *News of the World's* "accused was in a certain condition"): the water-closet is . . . I am not sure if I ever heard it mentioned; at school we called it the offie which must have been short for office. Then there are the many hush hush terms for natural functions of the Number One variety. At one time I used to be puzzled when the children in a nearby family whispered to their mother that they wanted to go to the House of Parliament. The coiner of that designation must have had a shrewd valuation of politics. It is primarily the women who guard the observance of the Sabbath. It is mother who sends the children to kirk and Sunday School: it is she who fears that the Devil will find mischief for idle hands to do—a tag, by the way, that must have had its origin in the masturbation Verbot. The mother is the home of Calvinistic morality, and the Fathers o' the Kirk must have been a sorry pack of old wives themselves.

In Scotland there is this particular circumstance of family life, that the mother rules through the father.

"Wait till your father comes home" is more often heard in Scotland than in England. I do not contend that women in England do not wear the trousers: what I do contend is that women in Scotland wear longer trousers. That may be the reason why men adopted the kilt—the masculine badge of feminity. It is a universal fact that every man identifies his wife with his mother. All men are more or less afraid of their wives because of this identification. So that when you have a strong character in women, as you assuredly do in Scotland, the male fear of the female is strong in proportion.

Hence in Scotland the psychologist often comes across a patient with an inverted Œdipus Complex. The Œdipus Complex in its baldest form postulates that the boy is in love with his mother and wants to get his rival father out of the way. The Elektra Complex is that in which the little girl wants to get rid of the rival mother. But, when the mother is obviously the power in the home, the emotions that would normally be attached to father become attached to mother. Symbolically, the boy will want to kill his mother and marry his father. We must remember that the mother is a much more important person than the father. Every child's first love is the mother:

the father only enters into the picture later. Gradually much of the love emotion that is given to the mother should be transferred to the father, but when the mother is too moral, too strict, too vampire-like, the childish emotion becomes fixated on the mother. In the case of a girl as in the case of a boy the reaction is thus:—the original love for mother, really a desire for love and security, changes into a form of hate, for man must hate what limits his freedom, what binds him. Life is growth and a powerful mother inhibits growth. And hate is inhibited love. Outwardly this may not be apparent. The son of twenty-five may appear to accept his mother's precepts and behests about late hours and women and drinking and smoking, but inside he is a rebellious raging fire.

Our schools do not touch psychology. They see children as pupils who are bright at maths. or dull at science, who are easy to manage or are disobedient. They see only shells. But the psychologist would see something else in one of our Scottish Academies or High Schools. He would see a crowd composed of individuals, each with his or her own bundle of fears and hates and loves and desires. He would notice the sheeplike respectable behaviour of the youthful Scots: he would mark their negative bearing, their acceptance of their narrow world without question. He would wonder what their homes were like, and if he knew their homes would ponder over them sadly, for a Scots suburban home is a place in which nothing of moment happens, a place in which nothing that matters is spoken of. Owing to the hush-hush home our secondary school pupils remain ignorant of the most interesting features of life. In homes where sex is taboo, where lying is a crime (when it isn't one of mother's white lies about her age or her having a headache, or one of father's white lies when he refuses to give a penny on the ground that ice cream is bad for one), where disobedience is a deadly sin, there must be in the children a host of repressions that are striving to find expression. The sex repressions try in vain to escape by means of lavatory writings and drawings, sex stories whispered in corners, ineffectual grubby sex adventures in dark closes. The "joy of life," as Oswald in Ibsen's *Ghosts* calls it, has no outlet in Scottish home or school. And that is why I say that all our boasted Scottish schooling is concerned with all that is valueless. The problem of Scotland is not a problem of schools: it is one of family life. It is psychological rather than educational. It is the problem of how Scotland can get rid of its clannish family tradition of camouflage and absence of emotion. The Englishman is notorious for his fear of expressing emotion, but compared with the Scot he is an emotional chatterbox. Scotland is an introverted country, able to extravert only in certain chilly lines, such as examinations and engineering and law. It has no art nor poetry, because such expressions would betray the feared emotions. Its peasantry, even in my boyhood days, had an emotional release in its dances, its reels and triumphs and schottisches, but I fear that today these have been overwhelmed by the foxtrot and waltz. The Scots dance was communal. It was only faintly sexual: you did not hold your partner close; you sweeled her on your arm and hooched lustily. The modern ballroom dance is sexual without much disguise and, without knowing what dancing in Scotland is today, I conjecture that a foxtrot, a waltz, or a tango in a village hall is badly danced. Ploughmen do not like sex to be too symbolic, and they are self-conscious about any expression of it. And the modern dance comes from and belongs to the bourgeoisie. It is the substitute for sex that moral and economic necessity requires. In a civilization in which sexual ripeness precedes by years economic ability to marry, and in which illegal sex is censured, the sexuality of the negro as expressed in jazz will give to dancing an exaggerated importance and a symbolic pleasure. The Scots countryside has lost its Reels o' Tulloch and has found nothing adequate to replace them. The Scots suburbs never had their reels and, looking to the south for all their motives, they accepted the imported jazz . . . with Calvinistic reservations, *vide* any Dornoch local paper. The Dornoch purists were logical. They realized that dancing to two in the morning was dangerous, because they grasped the awful truth that dancing is symbolic sexual intercourse.

I am no Freudian. I do not believe that sex is always the unconscious *Leitmotif* of life. I believe, however, that this business of suppressing sex is the chief occupation of Scotland. I believe that, fundamentally, the morality and authority of the Scottish mother aim at obviating the dangers of sex. I make no apology for returning to the subject of sex because I know that my readers have as great an interest in it as I have. Sexual intercourse has two objects: the unconscious object of carrying on the race, that is the fertility motive, and the conscious and partly unconscious object of pleasure. Sex repression applies to the pleasure object, not to the fertility object, so that, when writers connect the sexual freedom of the rustic with the fertility of the land, they are right in so far as the unconscious racial motive is concerned, but they ignore the individual unconscious and conscious motive. Only animals use sex biologically: man the "higher animal" is the only one that uses sex for pleasure. Yet why should not man use sex for pleasure? Why should he renounce what is far and away the most ecstatic pleasure of all? To sin in thought is often worse than to sin in deed. Scotland sins in thought. Conscious Calvinism must be accompanied by unconscious lasciviousness. There are no blacks and whites in life: there are only greys; no man is a saint and no man is a sinner. Burns had his religious longings and Knox had his carnal desires. It is this insane perversity to contrast opposites that is a special curse in Scotland. Insane, perverse, because there are no opposites in life: there are only complements.

The youth of Scotland are given an ideal of whiteness, of good, and they are given a dread of blackness, of evil. To give anyone an ideal is a criminal offence. The ideal of life should be to have no ideals. I think it was Sinclair Lewis who said that what interested him most in humanity was the fact that, after saying a dozen times that he won't have a whisky, a man finally does have a whisky. I subscribe to that statement. It is a man's weakness that makes him human and interesting. If Burns had been a strong man his name would have been dead by now. Weakness is more lovable than strength, and to fall into temptation is to fall into grace. This is no paradox, no attempt to shock. It is a firm conviction, a conviction born from the belief that mankind has saddled himself with an impossible ideal, which is expressed in the terms God, Truth, Honour, and the other deadly virtues. The only criterion of life is love, and the only aim is happiness. Scotland has much love, but it is love of wrong sort: it is possessive love, not creative love. It asks for but it does not give. Scotland deliberately seeks misery and death, because misery and death are the antithesis of life with its roses and songs. I have forgotten most of the songs I knew, and in trying to recall them I have a feeling that most of them concerned themselves with frustration and death. Even the lovely Border Ballads made death their theme. Scots songs dealt much with lost causes . . . I think of the *Four Maries, Bonnie Chairlie's noo awa*, and it is significant that the song of departure all the world over should be *Auld Lang Syne*. Only a backward-looking land that finds its glory in the past could produce a best seller like *Auld Lang Syne* . . . and now some interfering fool will prove to me that it was composed by an Englishman, I suppose.

It seems unfair to discuss the Scottish mother without touching on her husband, or as someone called him her better three-eighths. He is not so circumscribed by moral and social fears as his wife is, but being more of a baby than his wife is he is more self-centred. Mother will worry about how her bairns look and behave, and he will worry about personal social status. The Scot has a respect for civic or kirkly prominence, and his good name is better *with* riches. The inner Scotland is woman-made: the outer Scotland man-made. The man is, so to say, the window-dressing, not of much importance of course, but unfortunately he does not realize this. He may control the kirks and the railways and the cows, but his wife controls the soul of the nation—the children. He may be a bailie or an elder, but his wife chooses his suits for him. Drinking may be popular in Scotland because only at the bar has a man freedom from the careful, watchful eye of his womenfolk. Why the women ever allowed the convention that only low women entered pubs is curious: their control of their weak men would have been much stronger if they could have followed them into the bar parlours. Or maybe the convention represents man's last stand against his uplifter. The Scot has kept his women out of several departments of his life . . . his business, his politics, his pubs, his foregatherings at clubs and Masonic meetings. The sexes attract each other, but they are also antagonistic to each other. Man's unconscious homosexuality makes him found lodges and clubs in which he can be safe from the maternal eyes of women. Every man is at heart a timid boy, and a woman looks old sooner than a man because she *is* older . . . centuries older. She has a wisdom that man can never acquire, because she is God the creator.

How man succeeded in palming himself off as the superior being is the second greatest mystery in the world . . . the greatest mystery being the answer to the question: Why did man become a moralist? Man made the world as we know it. He built and dug and explored; he made a God in his own image and made himself God's priest; he made laws to defend man's property and laws to make women his property. He feared women, yet managed to give them an inferior status, and he doffs his hat to them as a token of recognition of that inferior status.

We can postulate theories of why this came about. Man was physically stronger than woman: when the dinner had to be slain it was the brawny man who threw the spear. When the fight for food and women came, the men slew each other violently. We can then argue that the logical conclusion of male superiority in muscle was that man made a civilization of men for men. A pleasant theory . . . until a still small voice whispers in our ear: "Then why do so many women wear the breeks?" No, we must try again.

We shall try brains. Man has a wider vision than woman: he can plan great bridges, giant ships, swift cars: he can think . . . Aristotle, Bacon, Carlyle, Marx, Bernard Shaw: he can create . . . Shakespeare, Milton, Rembrandt, Ibsen: he can destroy . . . Napoleon, Cæsar, Robespierre: he can build empires . . . Clive, Rhodes, Gordon. Women! Bah! What great women have lived? Cleopatra, Boadicea, Florence Nightingale, Queen Elizabeth, Jane Austen. How can woman create poems and pictures and empires when her creative instinct is fixed on the one act of creating a new life? Here we come to something important. Man cannot produce new life in himself, and the life force compels to produce new life outside himself. His empires and his ships are his babies. His maternal instinct made him glorify his offspring, and so it came about that men really in their hearts cared more for the things they made than for the children they fathered. A child is a company in which two people have shares, but a ship or a picture is motherless. That is why every woman is jealous of her man's creative activity. A woman with a pottering man hates his workshop, and a wife can be almost as jealous of a garden as of a mistress.

For the sake of argument let us say that man has a better brain than woman, that he pioneered and built and created because he could think more objectively, and it should be remembered that even in his physical make-up he is more objective than woman: his sexual apparatus is outside his body. This does not take us very far because brain is of less importance and of less strength than feeling or than instinct. All mass movements depend on emotion . . . the French Revolution, the Russian Revolution, Hitler Germany, Mussolini Italy, Calvinism. Movements that depend primarily on thought, such as Theosophy and Douglas Credit, never gain the support of the masses. Now man feels about objective things, woman about subjective things. Man is an extravert, woman an introvert. Man led the world because man was interested in the world. In my school I find that the boys are more interested in things, the girls more interested in people. I am beginning to see why I have intuitively linked up Capitalism with the father, and Communism with the mother. Capitalism is property, possession: Communism is lack of property, creation. There is equality between the sexes in Russia today, but tomorrow the woman may show that she is superior.

The world, then, is a man-made world because man had the power of being more objective than women, naturally, for every now and then the cave woman had to retire from her hunting or berry-picking to have a baby. And this reminds me of the telling fact that in Russia a pregnant woman, married or unmarried, retires to her cave with full-pay while she is bearing the child . . . but Marxist readers will surely feel like shouting indignantly that the motive is an economic one. No motive is unmixed, but in this case I feel that the chief motive is a deep respect for womanhood and childhood. Lucky is it for man that he can plant and build: his ability to be objective saves him from the fate of the male spider that is eaten by his Frau.

PSYCHOLOGY IN SCOTLAND

Man may conquer the world but he never conquers woman. True he exploits woman: in his wars for property he persuades woman to sacrifice her sons—his rivals: he makes them admire his struttings about in uniforms: he enslaves them in the East by force and in the West by the subtility of monopolising property: they accept their inferior position. In the ballroom they wait until a man asks them to dance: in the conservatory they wait for a man to propose . . . but their hidden preparation for the proposal is never revealed. No man ever proposes really: he is led up the garden path and he has to propose because his power is weaker than the woman's power, because he is a child, and every woman is his mother. There must be in woman a terrible hate and contempt for man, similar to the hate and contempt that domestic servants must have for their employers.

There must be a reason why woman accepts her inferior status, why she tolerates the ignominy of waiting to be asked to dance, why she is excluded from serving on a jury in a sexual trial, why she has to lay the table for idle brothers, why she is content with the worthless deference that consists of hat-lifting, door-opening, the whole gamut of " respect for woman ". And the reason must be that the smaller things are worth sacrificing for the greater things. One of the greatest things is the control of the emotions of humanity, and that the woman has, for humanity is made in the nursery. When the child leaves the nursery the main occupation of the woman is gone, and that may be a reason why the mothers " give their sons " to the cannon-fodder merchants of imperialism. " Woman's place is the home " and the grown-up son is of less interest than the child, and anyway, if war does not get him another woman will.

I have said that women are narrower than men. This is shown in the woman's contentment to rule the family. The larger family, the nation, she leaves to her men to make a kirk or a mill out of. And to return to Scotland, for the book is supposed to touch somewhat on Scotland, we see this narrowness of womanly outlook clearly. Mary Queen of Scots is still unconquered by the baleful lecturings of John Knox, but the Knoxes of this century have embittered her. Scottish women appear to be more on the defensive than English women are. Their octopus arms clutch their children because of a fear of . . . of what? Of Scotland and its hardness in money-making, its reverence for thought and learning, its insecurity as

PSYCHOLOGY IN SCOTLAND

a province . . . in short, fear of all that mere man has made of Scotland. The smaller the country the narrower are the women. Norwegian and Dutch women are like their Scottish sisters, undemonstrative and on the defensive. Woman in a large expanse like Russia are less protective and more *lebenslustig*. Yet we can apply the same reasoning to men. It was in the small countries that Calvinism took its strongest hold, or at least retained its hold longest. When I lectured six months ago in Oslo, my audience looked to me as if I had walked straight out of the pages of an Ibsen play. I grant that it was one of the most appreciative audiences that I have ever lectured to, that it showed an interest in modern education that no Aberdeen or Edinburgh audience would show, yet I had the strong feeling that, behind their modernity, lay a dark cloud of northern heaviness of spirit. It was only a feeling, and it is the feeling I often get in Scotland, a vague depressive emotion of being in a land that is stifling. Like any other feeling the root is bound to be subjective. Even when I lived in happy Bavaria, the sound of church bells of a Sunday made me feel depressed, because they had a direct association with the depression of a Scots Sabbath. It amounts to this that we can never be judges unless

PSYCHOLOGY IN SCOTLAND

we can be completely objective. What I could write about Japan after—say—a year's residence there would be of more value than anything I can write about Scotland. No man who has carved his initials on his home trees can ever see the wood for trees.

Returning to the title of this chapter I hold that psychology is badly needed in Scotland. With national psychology there is nothing to be done, but with individual psychology there is much to be done. If a battalion of psychologists could attack Scotland with the sole aim of rooting out the Calvinistic hatred of the flesh, the next generation might cease to find its joy of life abroad. The spirit is Scotland's curse, and the flesh is, alas, its burden. If only the sun would shine up north!

XII

SCOTLAND AND THE ENGLISH LANGUAGE

THERE is no Scots language. Gaelic is Celtic, and the so-called Scotch tongue is English with provincial pronunciation and provincial words. In England I have to avoid many words because I know they are unknown in the south. I cannot call a dish an ashet, a fork a graip, a turnip a neep, a house a biggin: I never tell a child to go ben the hoose: I never tie my pint when my shoe lace loosens. And I have found it convenient to drop Scotticisms like " whenever I saw him I knew that . . ." where the whenever should be " as soon as ". I never get a box of cigars " in a present ": I never have a shog in a swing: someone else is not " some other body ".

I have also had to modify my pronunciation, not only in such words as Ramsay MacDonald's worrrrld and the Burns Supper Burrrrns: I have had to change the Scottish letter i into an i. The tradition of Latin pronunciation in Scotland possibly gave us the Latin pronunciation of i. I was twenty before I learned that king should rhyme with ring. I was twenty-four when I first realized that my pronunciation of physician was physeecian. I gave up my pronunciations with reluctance, because we have a natural conservatism in matters linguistic. I always say "indīsputable" and the B.B.C.'s "indispūtable" annoys me: to hear "inexplicable" makes me squirm, for to me it will always be "inēxplicable," just as "tree" will always be "teree." But it shocks my ear to hear of someone "going to see a filum."

Scottish speech is slowly changing. My grandmother always "tint" her knitting when she mis-laid it; to her a window-pane was a "lozen." In my school days slate-pencil was "skillie," and a slice of bread was a "sheed o' loaf." No one said "good night," but when I was in a pub in Leuchars last summer I noticed that each departing rustic or railwayman said "good night," whereas thirty years ago they would have each said "guid nicht." This anglicising of dialect cannot be attributed to radio influence: the B.B.C. accent has only speeded up a transition that has been going on all the time. The coming of the motor car may have been the most potent factor in this anglicising of Scotland, for the motor car annihilated distance and remoteness. In

SCOTLAND AND THE ENGLISH LANGUAGE

olden days the people of a village seldom, if ever, left their immediate neighbourhood, and to this day there are people in towns who never move away from their own streets. A doctor in Blackfriars told me of an old woman patient of his, who had been born in Stamford Street, and had never been across the Thames to the Embankment, and there are probably many oldish people living in the Cowgate who have never walked along Princes Street . . . and, of course, there are many West Enders in Edinburgh who never saw the Cowgate and never will see it.

What is happening in Scotland is that the province is being made a suburb with a suburban speech. When a provost or bailie makes a public speech he drops his usual dialect and talks English. This fact has been used in the creation of a cycle of Scots language howlers, howlers of the kind told about an Edinburgh Lord Provost who had sat silent during a Council discussion on providing more urinals for the city. Finally someone said: " Let's hear whit the Provost has to say." The Provost growled: " Ach, to hell wi' more urinals: what the city needs is a few more arsenals." I fancy it was the same Lord Provost who objected to giving a retiring official an honorarium on the grounds that maybe the man couldna play it.

SCOTLAND AND THE ENGLISH LANGUAGE

I do not agree with some Scottish Nationalists who deplore the anglicising of northern dialect, just as I deplore those English old-timers who believe that by a process of revival they can make the English Folk Dance popular again. Setting the clock back may be a popular pastime in politics, but in the important things of life it is always unpopular. In spite of the present craze for intense nationalism, the future is one of internationalization. We are moving towards the World State, and the ambassadors are the important things that belong to the emotions. Today what is national is greed and militarism and language: today what is international is jazz and films and radio. To speak dialect all your days is to admit that you live in a small world: dialect is like the baby language of a home in which father is "Baba" or mother is "Lala"... the world outside speaks another language.

A critic has said that no Scot can write good English. That is not true. Scottish style may differ from English style; if anything it is more direct and plainer. It is less ornate, and it avoids the purple passage through fear of being meretricious. I can see no evidence that the laboured conscious style of Stevenson has influenced the literature of Scotland. In writing, as in speech, the tendency of Scotland is to call a spade a bloody shovel, and style as style is not over-valued. Stevenson had a notable syle, but to me he says hardly anything. Similarly Ruskin's prose style is delightful, although his message is unimportant. Style should be like music in the background: we should be consciously unaware of it. *The House of the Green Shutters* is a great book written in a great style, and its word-painting is felt before it is thought about. Consider its opening paragraph: "The frowsy chambermaid of the Red Lion had just finished washing the front steps. She rose from her stooping posture, and, being of slovenly habit, flung the water from her pail straight out, without moving from where she stood. The smooth round arch of the falling water glistened for a moment in mid-air. John Gourlay, standing in front of his new house at the head of the brae, could hear the swash of it when it fell. The morning was of perfect stillness." That is a picture that we can see, and even before we read in the next paragraph that Blowsalinda's petticoat is gaping behind we see her clearly for what she is. The book is full of such pictures, many of them painted with still better art.

What over-valuation of literary style there is in Scotland comes from the university influence. I do not know how much influence Professor Saintsbury

SCOTLAND AND THE ENGLISH LANGUAGE

had on Scottish literature during his long reign in the English department of Edinburgh University. I hope that influence was confined to a few, for, more than any other teacher I know of, did he make a separation between matter and style. He praised Blake for his poetry and Nietzsche for his prose style, but he dismissed their matter as matter written by madmen. I have heard him recite Coleridge's *Christabel* in tumtity-tums. On the whole, it is unlikely that "Old George" as we called him had much influence.

The universities and schools in general have had a big influence in emphasizing manner at the expense of matter. Grammar used to be one of the most important subjects in a Scottish school, and it probably still is. But grammar, like style, should be unconscious or at least foreconscious. Grammar is taking the stones of Cologne Cathedral to pieces to find out wherein the beauty lies. No man needs to know grammar consciously. Most of those who speak English most fluently could not tell you what parts of speech a "but" and an "also" are. Besides, grammar changes, or rather the uses of grammar change. It is no longer bad form to write a sentence that is without a predicate. It is no longer bad English to write: "Night. Black night. The stars gleaming."

SCOTLAND AND THE ENGLISH LANGUAGE

Scholastic emphasis on manner in writing is not confined to Scotland. Our whole educational system rates manner higher than matter, and a boy with neither brains nor imagination can pass an examination in English, if his prose is grammatical and fluent. The creative, as usual, is of minor moment. I have more than once said and written that it is better to compose a bad Limerick than to be able to recite *Paradise Lost* by heart.

Having forgotten all the Latin I ever knew, I make the tentative suggestion that the Latin teaching of Scotland may have influenced Scottish literature and speech, in what way I am too ignorant to say. I feel that Latin, a dead language, must have a deadening effect on children. Most children hate learning Latin or Greek, even more than they hate learning French or German: they possibly feel that the dead languages can never mean anything to them. The teaching of classics is one of the ugliest signs of civilisation's social insanity. Hardly any boy has the opportunity of going far enough to appreciate them: I stopped learning Greek just as I was beginning to find a little of the beauty of Homer. In schools the classics mean a dull grind in syntax and grammar. They are defended on several grounds, the feeblest of them being that, without Latin and Greek, how are we to know the meaning and derivation of words? The answer is: why should we? It doesn't help my life's happiness or my literary style to know that "treacle" is derived from the Greek *ther*, a wild beast, or better still that manufactured goods, made by machinery, owe their verbal adjective to Latin *factum*: to make, *manu*: by hand. The best defence of classics is that they bring us into touch with the great minds of long ago. Well, they just don't. Our children wade through oceans of grammatical mud, and they never even glimpse the sun-kissed mountains we call Cicero and Virgil and Horace and Homer. Just before they cross their last muddy stream, they are beckoned to, and they gladly start on another muddy tramp—to offices and mills and universities.

Scotland's love for Latin springs from its ecclesiastical past. The vogue, that Latin has had in Scotland, never had the aim of reaching up to the great Roman authors: its aim was to reach down to the dog Latin of the priests. The progress of a nation can be gauged from its attitude to Latin and Greek. In England their strongholds are the Public Schools, that is, the least forward-moving institutions in the land.

SCOTLAND AND THE ENGLISH LANGUAGE

It is probable that the teaching of Latin in Scotland has more effect on the mind than on literary style. At any rate, as a colossal waste of time it is unapproachable. Language is a means to an end. Its end should be to be able to read the masters of old, or to speak to foreigners of today. By making Latin a mere exercise in gerunds and datives Scotland made of a dead language a dead incubus. Grammar is a scaffold and Scotland decorated the scaffold and forgot about the building.

In writing about Scotland and the English Language I feel that I ought to say something about the Press in Scotland. I have seen so little of it in recent years that any comments I can make will be limited. Some years ago the Scottish newspaper was, compared with the English newspaper, austere: it eschewed sensationalism: it was solid almost to dullness. If an earthquake swallowed up half of Asia *The Scotsman* announced the fact in sober headlines. *The Glasgow Herald*, though not so conservative as *The Scotsman*, was just a shade heavy. But the *Glasgow Evening News* and the *Edinburgh Evening Dispatch* were, and still are, two bright cheerful antidotes to the respectability of their morning sisters.

It is pleasant to speculate why an evening paper

has always been less heavy than a morning paper. We keep our lighter moments until evening, not only because evening frees us from work: there is more to it than that. Each day is a life. We are re-born each morning, and our reluctance to rise at the alarum clock's hateful call is our dislike of being born. No man is at his best in the morning. The funniest story told before breakfast would leave me cold. Our mornings are our waking times, and we awake slowly. But as our life-day goes on we grow up, and by the evening we are beginning to enjoy our middle-age. Death, the night, is approaching: let us eat, drink, and be merry, because the life-day is short.

The evening paper is lighter in tone because man is lighter in spirit at the end of the day. He is less responsible, and his irresponsible evening paper fits in with his mood. On the other hand, man is jaded in the evening, jaded because his life-day has not come up to his expectations, and the evening paper attempts to cheer him up artificially by giving him sensational news. When a man has worked hard from nine o'clock until six, he does not want to concentrate on political leaders as he journeys to his home in the suburbs. The sensational Press flourishes because the weight of industrialism makes thinking a burden, and a pictorial Press flourishes best in a civilization in which work is dreary and hard. The successful newspaper today must appeal to the eye rather than to the head.

Now we see this process in later-day Scottish journalism. The *Scotsman* and *The Glasgow Herald* provided food for thought for the people who liked thought, the people who judged a sermon by its thought. Today Scotland still has its native morning papers, but it also has its pictorial and sensational " Northern Editions " of English papers, and skilfully made they are, with their ITALY AND SANCTIONS in one column, and their DEATH OF MEARNS FARMER, in the neighbouring column. I wish I knew how the invasion of the yellow Press has affected the circulation of our old staid dailies.

Scottish journalism is good in spite of the fact that Lengs and Thomsons are used as platforms on the main line to Fleet Street. Why the Scot should have a talent for journalism it is not easy to say, nor am I certain that it is a worthy talent to have. Journalism is often prostitution: I know men of left-wing sympathies who have to write diehard drivel. Journals today, like the theatre of today, are commercial propositions. Their circulation is their first concern, and their censorship excludes everything that might offend an advertiser. Besides most of them are attached to a political power, and what is not muzzled by the advertisement is muzzled by the political boss. Hence the successful journalist must be he who best increases the circulation. I hate to think that the Scot should be the best man to make wealth for the newspaper dictator or for the pill advertiser, but judging by the accent of Fleet Street he apparently is. It would be a sad day for English commercialism and exploitation if Scotland went off the map literally as well as metaphorically. The grouse moors, the Press, and now the English railway. Poor Scotland.

Can it be that the Scot has the psychology of the servant? He serves his Harmsworths and Beaverbrooks well, but does he serve himself well? Are we all at heart Hielan' ghillies? It almost looks as if we have spent a few centuries recompensing England for Edward I's failure to exploit Scotland. Our native land withstood the armed bands of Edward, but it cannot withstand the peaceful penetration of monopoly capital.

So let us give up our claims to be the superior partner in the Union of the Crowns. Let us realize that our Engish tongue has automatically made us dependent on England, that England takes from us many of our best men. Our only chance of becoming a self-respecting nation is through the formation of a Socialist world, a world in which goods will be made for use and not for profit, a world where our clever lads will not have to sell their journalistic talent for money, a world in which man will be of more importance than goods that sell. A Nationalist Scotland I do not want to see, and a Soviet Scotland I know I am most unlikely to see. But, lads, a Soviet Scotland wud be a gey braw placie.

XIII

HEALTH, MANNERS, AND DISCIPLINE

It may be said that health and manners ought to be left to the home. They usually are, unfortunately. There seems to be a general assumption that a woman knows by instinct exactly how to bring up a child physically and psychologically. Such an assumption is a dangerous one: animals may know by instinct what is best for them in the way of food, but humans assuredly do not. So in behaviour, a cat may have a good idea of what a kitten ought to be, but a human mother dare not know what her child ought to be.

Consider Scottish food. By the palate's taste it is excellent food. A Forfar bridie is delicious: the cream-cakes and cheese-cakes of Scotland are food for the gods: kail made with a marrow bone and grated carrots is better than any soup ever made. The temptation to overeat in Scotland is a great one. From a health point of view, however, Scottish food is dangerous. There is a superfluity of starch, and an

HEALTH, MANNERS, AND DISCIPLINE

insufficiency of fruit and vegetable. White bread is still national, so national that I always have difficulty in buying a wholemeal loaf in most Scottish towns. If Scotland has heard of vitamins her bakers' shops do not betray the fact.

Now feeding is of infinitely greater importance than schooling. It is more vital that a nation should know about proteins than about prose, yet I do not have any evidence that food figures in the school curriculum in Scotland . . . or elsewhere. In Scotland too much has been taken for granted in the food question. The nation has had a good reputation for healthy and stalwart men and women, men and women reputed to have thriven on brose and porridge. In my boyhood days a Forfarshire ploughman had his wages and his meal and milk. He used all three. Today I am told that he sells his meal and milk, and buys canned food and white bread.

The middle classes appear to be following modern ideas about food, if one can judge by the number of fruit shops that continue to spring up in every town; but the working classes do not have any knowledge about food values . . . not that that knowledge would help a family on the dole very much. I think, however, of the children in a village. It would do no harm to cut out a lesson or two on decimal fractions, and give a lesson on the evils of the cold ham type of high tea, or the poisonousness of " infused " tea.

I know from experience that children are more interested in food than in anything else. When our self-government meeting begins to flag I sometimes get up and make the proposal that second helpings be abolished. The meeting awakes to life, gets to its feet . . . and yells angrily. Freud is wrong in holding that sex rules our lives: it isn't sex; it is food. And a lesson on food would make the worst dunce take an intelligent interest.

Why then should so great an interest be neglected in our schools? I wonder is it because food, like politics, is a controversial subject? It is, you know, for hundreds of commercial men are thundering out newspaper advertisement-lies daily, lies that declare that their food is the best. It is highly probable that if the Scottish Education Department were to advise teachers to preach the excellence of wholemeal bread, the millers of white flour would rise in fury and bring the matter up in Parliament. Only in a non-profit system can food be considered as food and not as something to sell. It is only in our mad system that coffee and herrings can be dumped in the sea because there is no sale for them. In Russia they send loads of black currants from the south to Archangel region, because black currants contain much vitamin C, and there is a deficiency of this vitamin in the north. And now that Russian science has discovered that dog-hips and pine needles contain still more vitamin C, it is possible that the north will be able to produce its own C. Only a system that eliminates profit can treat food as a necessity for all.

I see a difficulty in including food in the school curriculum. It would require a teacher of Herculean nerve to give a lesson to Glasgow or Dundee children on food values. The physical condition of the poor in these cities is appalling. When I took English friends to see Edinburgh Castle I blushed to see their expressions as they looked at the sentries: they were all diminutive bantam battalion lads, apparently recruited from the slums of industrialism. Teaching on food is really a beginning at the wrong end. Ignorance of food is bad, but shortage of food is hellish . . . and although the Scottish dominie has his faults, he did not make the industrial revolution.

I am not sure that I should introduce drink into the curriculum if I were made Educational Dictator of

HEALTH, MANNERS, AND DISCIPLINE

Scotland. For one thing children would not be directly interested in whisky and beer, and for another, the evils of drink lie in the social weaknesses that drive to drink. Strong drink is an evil, only when the reality of life is unbearable, and most of us are sober because our immediate reality does not make us desperate. No, I think the drink question might well be left out. And there is this factor, that on a " balanced diet " a man has less desire to take alcohol. It would be an interesting, if cruel, experiment to try to cure a drunkard by feeding him on fruit only for six weeks.

Manners, I am glad to say, do not come into the Scottish curriculum. True, we have the infantilely stupid system of making children address teachers as " Sir," of making them request permission to " leave the room," but these inanities belong more to discipline than to manners proper. There isn't much wrong with Scottish manners. The Scots' etiquette may be weak, but their manners are strong. Etiquette is conscious: manners unconscious. Etiquette accompanies class distinction. The village blacksmith does not lift his cap to the school charwoman. I recall a parish minister who had an elaborate code of graded greetings. To the laird's wife his hat came off with a flourish; the dominie's wife made the hat rise about six inches from the head; the grocer's wife got a rise of an inch, the joiner's wife half an inch. There the hat-lifting came to an end. To the school charwoman he raised a finger, and to Jean, the servant at the manse, he gave a mere nod. A walk through the village with him was a liberal education.

There is a sincerity about the Scot that makes him suspicious of etiquette, not only suspicious but almost contemptuous. Uppishness is not approved of, unless, of course, in Kelvinside, although in every town there are women of the type of the mother who took her boy to the Zoo. He clutched his mother's skirt and cried: " Mither, mither, look at the bloody elephant!" His mother got very red. " Angus," she said severely, " don't point."

It is true that a little coaching in etiquette might obviate a few of the awkward moments we Scots have when we go into " society ". I squirm when I think of my first dinner party at the age of nineteen, when I used a spoon . . . and found the others were using forks. I recall with mixed feelings my introduction to finger bowls . . . but I did not drink from mine. It is strange that a table bloomer brings more shame than any other social bloomer. The story of

HEALTH, MANNERS, AND DISCIPLINE

George Morrow's diner in *Punch*, who said to the waiter: "Take away that gentleman's soup; I can't hear the band" has had as large a vogue as any sex story. I am sure that we have food repressions that are similar to sex repressions.

Yes, our schools might have a special etiquette class for climbers, but if we did, some idiot would give us a *Social Behaviour Primer, Book I*, full of descriptions of how to address a bishop, and how to behave when presented at court. Writers of school textbooks have a talent that is almost a genius for irrelevance.

The discipline of Scottish schools is no better and no worse than that of other schools. School discipline is an anachronism that will disappear only when our civilization requires the only discipline that has any value—the discipline of an orchestra or a football team. Our city schools are barracks, and in barracks one must have the wrong kind of discipline . . . fear, instead of love. All praise to the many teachers in cities like Glasgow and Edinburgh, who, in spite of their prison buildings, manage to give their pupils a discipline that is one of love.

One good feature of discipline in Scottish schools is that it ends with the completion of the school career. A boy in Peebles addresses his teacher as

"Sir," just as a boy in St Albans does, but the St Albans boy, when he leaves school, addresses his boss as "Sir", while the Peebles boy doesn't address his boss as anything. This is as it should be. School discipline is an artificial thing. Bobby does not address his teacher as "Sir" because his teacher is necessarily a man deserving respect: he does so because he knows that he has to. When the outward compulsion ends with school leaving, Bobby recognizes that the "Sir" meant nothing at all, and he drops the word from his vocabulary. The English boy keeps using the word all his life.

I may appear to be quibbling over this use of the word "Sir." Folks cry: "What does it matter if you call a man "Sir" or not?" I answer that it matters a lot, because the "Sir" is a symbol of a false servility . . . or is it a true sevility? It signifies that men have different levels in life, and I hold that levels should not be labelled. They should not be on a cash or class basis, and here, for perhaps the only time in this book, I think the majority of Scots will be with me. As a race we abhor servility and toadying. As a race we have everything necessary for a great democracy . . . and we are a province of England, servile, deferential England. That's a gey paradox, lads. It is more than that: it is the Sphinx riddle of the North. Fundamentally, it may be a question of character versus economic power. But it is sad to think that the only thing England could not rob Scotland of was its inability to bow the knee visibly.

XIV

THE FUTURE

THE future of Scottish education depends wholly on the future of Scotland as a nation. Education to a nation is what whitewash is to a house: the house would stand without the whitewash, and the nation would stand without its schools. The people who make a nation thrive are its practical men, working certainly under the guidance of theoreticians, and as school subjects are of small importance to theoreticians, I conclude that the practical men of Scotland would carry on thrivingly without any M.A.'s or B.Sc.'s. Not that I undervalue science; what I undervalue is the science of schools and universities that, like Latin, stops short before the great goal is achieved. At the university I passed my degree in Chemistry with a paper that must have been somewhere about 90 per cent. I liked the subject, and knew it well. Today I know nothing about it. I did not pursue my chemical studies further because other things interested me more, and that is precisely what is happening at schools and

THE FUTURE

universities—a smattering of chemistry, of Latin, of History, and a hall-mark degree or certificate at the end of it. A degree that deceives, as in the case of my own degree in Honours English: my opinions on Spenser and Milton aren't worth giving to a class of infants: my appreciation of poetry is on a level with a slum-dweller's appreciation of Hegel's philosophy.

Naturally if you crowd a dozen subjects into a school curriculum you turn out half-educated citizens. I repeat that all any school needs in the way of subjects is teaching in reading, writing, and counting—counting up to twenty is almost enough: the rest will follow unconsciously. I repeat that the rest should be creative work of hand and eye and ear. Our spoon-fed curriculum is a waste of time and of juvenile life.

The future of Scottish education depends on the future of Great Britain. It is a servant that only cleans the boots of the master. The City could change the future of Europe at any moment, say, if it decided to finance the U.S.S.R. instead of Germany. And the future of Europe is the future of Scotland. Our little university degrees have as much control over world revolution as the proverbial fly on the wheel has over the wheel's revolution. Our youth is kept grinding at geometry while the world outside the schoolroom walls is volcanic and explosive.

There are only two powerful forces in the world today—capital and labour, master and servant, rich and poor. Scotland is a small part of the world that is ruled by the rich and powerful, and, so long as they continue to rule, Scottish education will be what it is today—a shadow. As I write the National Government has been returned with a large majority. That means that the masses support Capitalism and the *status quo*. It may mean a foreign policy aimed at uniting Capitalism against Soviet Russia, or it may mean internecine war between imperialist countries (note the tension between Italy and Britain over imperial possessions). Capitalism leads to war because Capitalism is profit, and profit means competition, and in the last resort competition is one of force, that is war. So that the immediate fate of Europe is rivalry and war.

And Scottish education? What does it matter what our schools are like if our civilzation is putrid? How can we stop a war by teaching Latin or employing school dentists? How can we lessen unemployment by establishing cookery rooms? We can formulate a neat little problem in arithmetic:—If the power of

THE FUTURE

a Mussolini is 99.9 per cent., what power has a teacher in a Brindisi elementary school? Indeed we might introduce topical questions into our arithmetic test cards. . . . If munitions £1 shares stand at 135s. 6d., what is the market value of an M.A. degree? I could think of many questions for all school subjects. If a child whose father is on the dole lives well on two shillings a week, write a short essay defending the feeding of foxhounds. Or again: Who won the Great War and what did he win? If the people who make subtle propaganda in the schools with their Empire Days have any sense of fair play, they should not object to questions of the above type. I hasten to say that such questions would have just about as much ultimate effect as the propaganda in false patriotism, for propaganda does not make movements: it steps in to support a movement that has taken place. I say ultimate effect. Evil propaganda will make a generation die for rich men's pockets; it will help to prolong a monopoly, but propaganda does not make a mass movement. Such a movement springs from a great economic need. Britain will sweep away its unequal civilization only when it feels that it is unbearable. Propaganda appeals to consciousness, and movement comes from an unconscious desire. Hence

THE FUTURE

in an ideal school there would be no propaganda. Children ought not to be taught to salute either the Union Jack, or the Red Flag, or the Hackenkreuz. It is criminal to use children as a support for our passing styles of living. A Russian mother took her boy away from my school on the ground that, since coming to me, he had " lost all interest in the State." I said to her: " If a boy of twelve had any interest in the State I should call him a mentally deficient." We had a Russian girl of seven who wrote her father saying that her reading lessons were bad because there was no Marxism in them. In this case the father was wise enough to deplore her opinion.

Now the least discerning reader will have gathered by this time that I prefer Communism to Capitalism. But I value child nature more than either, and to impose anything, even when it is what I consider good, on a child, is to me an evil thing. To me it is like tempting a child to drink gin. It is indeed tempting a child to drink gin, and the adult, who is an addict to alcohol, is like an adult whose childhood's propaganda gin has become a formed habit.

Our attempts at living are tentative, and it is right that we should try to solve our own problems. It is wrong, however, to attempt to include the children in this solution, because the new generation will have its own problems to solve later. By emasculating them by our propaganda we are fixing our problems on them, so that, in their adulthood, they will be perpetuating the old problem of their parents, instead of looking for a new solution of life's difficulties. The world is not going to stop at Fascism; it is not going to stop at Communism. Possession which is Fascism, and creation which is Communism will go on struggling to improve their positions, go on possibly for ever, for in every man there is the conflict between having and doing.

I hold, therefore, that the chief subject in any school should be psychology, that is the study of human behaviour. Children should be taught to realize what they are as individuals, and later, what they are as social units. The objective world is subjective: each man is an Italian and an Abyssinian, a Communist and a Fascist, an "Aryan" and a Jew. Propaganda encourages one half and beats up the other half. If we could so educate our children that they understood their own complexities, humanity would go on to peace and creation.

It is significant that in ending this book I have got far away from Scotland. We can only see Scotland as a part, and a very small part, of world civilization. Its system of education is only a part of a universal system of education. Yet it is a pity that the part Scotland now plays is such a minor one, pity that Scotland is just a corner of England. A small country, like a small man, has an inferiority complex, and unfortunately, quantity counts for more than quality these days. The millions of Russia and Germany and China can make history, can alter the face of the globe, and the small Scotlands and Hollands and Denmarks have to adapt themselves to the world as it is made by the big battalions.

So, instead of troubling about the schooling of Ecclefechan, let us look forward to the world that the powerful nations are making for us. That is, let us cease to be national and begin to think internationally. The thing that matters most to humanity is to make life happier and more creative. Concentrating on schools and universities will not help to further that aim. Only psychological and economic freedom can bring about a world that is happy and creative: only brotherly love can rid the world of war and hate and crime.

I wish I could return in a thousand years to see what education has done for Scotland . . . and the world.

XV
BOOK REVIEW

It is time that the monopoly of book-reviewing was attacked. The author is bound to know more about his book than any reviewer knows, and therefore I propose to start a new fashion of book-reviewing by authors. Here goes:

Scotland and Education, by A. S. NEILL (Routledge, 5s. net).

The author of this book reminds one of the schoolboy who was to be examined on the History of India. He was not a hard-working boy, but he had some imagination. He was certain that there would be a question on Clive in the exam. paper and he concentrated on Clive's life. But the paper asked about Warren Hastings. The boy was put out at first, but a brain wave settled his difficulty. He began:

"Warren Hastings' life can only be understood if we know the life of the other great Indian pioneer Clive. Clive was born on——"

BOOK REVIEW

The boy passed, but we are not so sure that a fair examiner would pass Mr Neill's book on Scotland. Obviously his knowledge of Scottish History is as inadequate as his knowledge of modern Scotland. He has used his Clive very effectively, although who or what his Clive is, it is not easy to guess. His Clive almost looks like a composite figure made up of Freud, God, and the Devil. He has made a round box and then tried to fit a square Scotland into it. In other words he has looked at Scotland with eclectic eyes (a good phrase: other reviewers please copy). Scotland is not the depressing place he pictures it. He has deliberately selected only those colours that suit his gloomy landscape. He has deliberately ignored the noble band of artists and men of action who have proved to the world the glory of Scotch education. Names of fame do not enter his pages: Henryson, Dunbar, Kennedy, Ramsay, Hogg, Watt, Carnegie, Lauder, Balfour. He shows no appreciation of Scott, and his appreciation of Burns is a perverted pseudo-psycho-analytical one. He quotes Grant's *History of the Burgh Schools*, but he scarcely shows that he has read it. He says nothing about the history of music in Scotland, a history that is one of the brightest spots in an admittedly sunless land. He does not even relate the fine part that Scotsmen have played in British politics, and it is almost certain that he does not know the number of Prime Ministers who have come from his own country.

He says some true things about Scotland but he leaves out a thousand true things that are a credit to Scotland. Scotland's educational system has been famous for two generations at least, and its elementary education has been of a higher quality than the elementary education in the south, so that a Dorset labourer is a more ignorant man than a Midlothian ploughman. When we consider that in one of his earlier books the author confessed to being two places from the bottom of the list in the Normal School Entrance Examination, we naturally take with a grain of salt his bitter criticisms of the Leaving Certificate. There is a hint of sour grapes here. Moreover, in this book there is a strong suggestion of chagrin at not having obtained the recognition in Scotland that he desired. His native town keeps him in his place, pretends not to know him. Scotland does not send him pupils.

His book is disappointing, but most books on Scotland are. Of recent years there has been an outcrop of books on Scotland, and without exception thay have all missed the bus. They have all been too parochial, too selective. A really good History of Scotland has never been written. All these modern writers have bees in their bonnets; they use Scotland as a sprig of heather to feed their own particular bee. Scotland needs an historian who has a hive of bees in his bonnet, bees that will settle on the thistles of Roxburgh and the heather of Ross and even seek for honey in Mr Neill's hated Calvinism. Scotland is greater than its sons.

Nevertheless, in spite of its drawbacks, its ignorance of Scottish life, its extreme prejudices, its over-valuation of Bavarian and Russian Arcadias, the book is worth reading. The author's style is not literary: he has no purple passages, no talent for painting in words as the author of *The House with the Green Shutters* had. It almost seems to be modelled on the plain style so much admired by his teacher, the late George Saintsbury. Yet it is a serviceable style without padding. The author says what he means and says it clearly, even when what he means means nothing at all.

For Product Safety Concerns and Information please contact our EU
representative GPSR@taylorandfrancis.com
Taylor & Francis Verlag GmbH, Kaufingerstraße 24, 80331 München, Germany

www.ingramcontent.com/pod-product-compliance
Lightning Source LLC
Chambersburg PA
CBHW061832300426
44115CB00013B/2346